Out
of the
Fire

Out of the Fire

Tameka Smith

Designed by D′ Technology

Published by D.O.R.M. International Publishing

A Christian Publisher located in Atlanta, Georgia (USA)

Visit our website at **www.dormpublishing.com**

Printed in the United States of America

First Edition: April 2023

ISBN-13: 978-1-957038-08-7

ISBN-10: 1-957038-08-X

D.O.R.M

DEDICATION

This book is dedicated to my mother Rose Marie Smith and my three children Jarret, Walter, and Maya.

ACKNOWLEDGMENTS

To GOD be all of The Glory for not only making it possible for me to write this book but for Him being The Author of my life's story.

I know that GOD strategically placed each one of these individuals in my life at the right times & I want to Thank you all for your love, support, assistance, expertise, professionalism, encouragement, wisdom, guidance, and for your prayers along my journey.

GOD
My mother Rose Smith
Great Grandmother Annie Mae Parris
Aunt Connie Blair
My mentor Saundra Phillips
Gary and Karen Miller
Bishop Gary and sister Frenchie Wright
Pastor Hamilton and First Lady Hamilton
Good friend Harry Davenport
Dr. Derashay, Kingdom Strategist, Publisher
Denise Walker, Editor
Childhood friend Temecka Smith
Good friend Rhonda Gallman
Photographer Sabrina Turner of Euphoric Phrames

Table of Contents

PROLOGUE

December 28, 2021

"IT'S TIME, IT'S TIME TO WRITE YOUR BOOK, TAMEKA." I heard GOD clearly speak these words to me while I was sitting in my car at work. I was on my 3-hour lunch break, one day before my forty-eighth birthday.

"Nobody can tell your story better than you. It was never meant for anyone else to write your story but you. That's why it didn't work out each time you tried to get someone to help you write it," God continued.

He went on to give me names of people and instructions on how to reach out to them. God had already selected these individuals and gave them the spirit to assist me. Finally, he gave me a publishing company who would then agree to take on my autobiography.

Prior to that, I had approached 3 different people with book writing experience to take my journal notes and put them into a storyline for me.

I had never written a book before, and I didn't think I could do it on my own, cause it to be successful, and deliver the message intended to people who needed it.

GOD SAW IN ME WHAT I COULDN'T, AND HE KNEW THE PLANS HE HAD FOR ME AND THIS BOOK.

WHENEVER GOD calls you to do something, do it with confidence, knowing HE HAS ALREADY EQUIPPED YOU FOR THE TASK.

He had already given me the storyline.... I just needed to tell it at the appointed time.

Generational Curses and Perseverance...

CHAPTER 1

I was born in Knoxville, Tennessee on Dec 29, 1973, to my beautiful mother Rose. She was only 14 when she had my oldest brother. Four years later she had me. Six years after that, she had my baby brother Christopher.

Rose Marie, as I often jokingly call her, did her very best raising us in a single parent home in The College Homes Housing Project. We were like any other typical black family that lived there at the time. We didn't have a lot of money, but we never went to bed hungry or without decent clothes on our backs and shoes on our feet.

Speaking of shoes, remember those black and white or brown and white Buster Brown's? Yea, those. I absolutely hated those shoes and would cry whenever my mom would tell me to wear them.

I was rough on shoes and would tear up a pair of new shoes within a month. Although it was never intentional, I'd be kind of happy when they would tear up, so I wouldn't have to wear them anymore. Nope, not my mama. She'd buy me another fresh pair. I just wanted to scream, "I'm not wearing them...." But I knew better. I wanted to live to see another day.

Writing about this now is hilarious. Yes, Mama, I hated them that much. I'm sorry, but thank you anyway, sweetheart.

My mother worked hard, and she was so determined to make a better life for herself and her children. Because she was a high school dropout, she knew it would hinder her from future job or career opportunities, so she studied for and earned her GED. After obtaining her GED, She initially applied to The University of Tennessee but was denied because she didn't have enough high school credits.

That didn't deter her. She applied for and started going to Pellissippi Community College where she excelled and later graduated Magnum Cum Laude. My mother then matriculated on over to The University of Tennessee where she obtained a master's degree in social work and graduated at the top of the Dean's List. Mama later pursued her PH.D. in public health online.

I always thought my mother was beautiful, extremely intelligent, and very articulate, but it's her resilience that I admired the most. She was the first from her generation to go to college and earn multiple degrees and the first to buy a home. I aspire to be as successful as her some day! I don't think she truly knows the positive impact she's had on me or how proud of her I've always been.

Everything you're going to read about the traumatic experiences of my life was absolutely no fault of my mother.

I thought it was important to share that information about my mother, so you would hold off on prematurely passing judgement about her once you read my story. Everything you're going to read about the traumatic experiences of my life was absolutely no fault of my mother.

She never knew because I never told a soul, and she didn't find out until later in my adult life. Her pain of finding out was the equivalent of the pain she would've felt had I told her as a child. I may not have my mother had I told her anything back then while it was happening. She would probably be in prison for murder. Therefore, I do not regret keeping any of it a secret, and I'd do it all over again the same way just to protect her!

My mom had six siblings (four brothers and two sisters). My grandmother was a hardworking single mother as well. She, too, had her first child when she was barely a teenager and was also a high school dropout. We were close to our grandmother. We called her "Mama." Oh, how I miss her.... Mama (Grandmother) was a short woman with beautiful skin and an hourglass shape. She had the softest, prettiest, tiny feet you'd ever want to see. Mama took care of her feet. She used that back in the day product *Fancy Hands and Feet*.

After work she'd say, "Come and rub your grandma's feet...." I used to love rubbing and massaging my grandmother's feet after her long, hard day of work because they were baby soft, and I loved her with all my heart.

When the holidays would come, my grandmother and her youngest and closest sister, Sarah Gene, would get together and do most of the cooking. The rest of the family would all go to my aunt Sarah's house to gather and celebrate the holidays and enjoy my grandmother's famous potato salad. NOBODY MADE POTATO SALAD LIKE MAMA, AND TIL THIS DAY, I'VE YET TO FIND ONE THAT EVEN COMES CLOSE.

There'd be so much food, laughter, and kids would be all over the place. Those were the happier times... But along with the happy times, there were a lot of unhappy times.

All my uncles, one of my aunts, and some of my older cousins struggled with drug addiction, mental illness, and were always in and out of prison.

Back then, the words rehabilitation and mental health were never spoken in the Black community or at least not in my family. The only glimpse of help available was prison and jail, and they spent a lot of time in and out of those places.

I remember them nearly worrying my poor grandmother to death. The police would often come to her home searching and looking for those boys whenever they'd get into trouble. They'd steal from her all the time. It had gotten so bad that she had to eventually place a padlock on her bedroom door to keep them out. Unfortunately, it didn't work...I remember seeing one of my uncle's kick her bedroom door in while she was at work. He searched for money or something he could steal and trade for drugs.

Another time, one of my uncles was on a crazed drug binge. Because Grandmother wouldn't let him into the house, he shattered her kitchen window by putting his whole arm through it with one punch. They were forever doing something to cause my grandmother stress and grief. Yet, I don't remember ever seeing or hearing her cry. I'm sure she did. She just never did in front of us.

Grandmother later met a gentleman, moved away to Chattanooga Tennessee, and got married. We were extremely sad about her moving away. She was a large part of all we knew. We were at her house just as much as we were at our own, and all of that changed forever. She moved away and had a beautiful wedding in the backyard of her new home. Her wedding colors were white and powder blue, and I was a flower girl.

Mama was glowing with joy and peace as she walked down the aisle. Looking back, I'm glad she left and moved away from her troubled adult children. She deserved to be at peace, happy, loved, and out of public housing. I later went to visit her one summer and experienced one of the most pivotal times of my life.

Grandma might've moved away, but those generational curses of addiction, teen pregnancy, dropping out of school, prison, jail, and mental illness were still here and passing on generation to generation.

Earlier Encounters with God!

CHAPTER 2

As a little girl, I had an imaginary friend I called Basha. I talked to it every day, so much that my oldest brother would tease me about it, all the way up to my adult years. He would occasionally call me and ask, "Tameka have you talked to Basha lately?"

I would reply, "No, I haven't talked to ole Basha lately."

We'd both start laughing.

I don't know why, as a 6-year-old child, I named my imaginary friend such an odd and uncommon name. As I got older, I would often wonder why I identified with my imaginary friend by that name and why it has stuck with me for years.

It wasn't until I started doing my research as an adult that I discovered what the name actually means. Basha is a Hebrew girl's name, and it means "Good tidings, daughter of God." I was shocked, blown away, overwhelmed, and but happy to discover that.

There I was a little black girl from the hood who had never heard of, let alone ever spoken a single word of Hebrew, yet I identified with this imaginary friend by a Hebrew name with such a powerful and spiritual meaning.

So, I'm not sure if it was the Holy Spirit saying "Basha" to me, meaning Good tidings daughter of God or if it was my guardian angel. Whatever the case, I don't see that as being a coincidence at all! God is such a mystery, and that was definitely a mysterious experience.

GLORY TO GOD!

I also remember my experiences going to church with my great grandmother, Annie Mae Parris. She taught me more in depth about the Lord.

Nanny was holiness. She didn't drive, so a white van picked us up for church whenever I'd stay over her house.

Whenever I stayed at Nanny's, I was sure to go to Bible study and church every Wednesday and Sunday, no ifs ands or buts about it. She was a devoted follower of Christ, the same behind closed doors as she was in front of other people. Nanny never wore pants, and I never heard worldly music playing on her radio or T.V.'s.

Nanny had a gift of discerning things in the Spirit, and she'd often prophesy over me as a little girl, as a teenager, and as a young adult. As a little girl, she would tell me I had a gift, and I had been called and chosen, She'd say God was going to use me mightily for His Kingdom. She continuously told me what she saw in me until her passing.

One Sunday, as we were waiting for the church van, a dog approached Nanny and began to growl at her. He showed his teeth aggressively. Nanny was not afraid. She pointed her finger at that dog and said, "I REBUKE YOU, IN THE NAME OF JESUS." That dog made a high pitch yap, lowered its head, and walked off slowly, wagging its tail. That was powerful. It showed me there's power in the name of Jesus, and demons tremble at the sound of that name!

> I instantly fell to my knees, began to weep, and cried out, "Oh Lord, please forgive me."

As I grew older, I began dreaming dreams. I remember two dreams I had in my younger adult life so vividly. It's as if I dreamt them yesterday. I would always call Nanny whenever I had a dream I didn't understand so she could interpret it for me.

My first vivid dream about Jesus happened when I was 19 years old. I was living in my second apartment, and I dreamt that loud trumpets were playing. The trumpets were playing so loud that they awakened me. I ran down my steps, opened my front door, and saw the sky split down the middle, and Jesus was walking on the clouds. His eyes were red as fire, and He was dressed in all white garments. I instantly fell to my knees, began to weep, and cried out, "Oh Lord, please forgive me."

Jesus looked at me and said, "It's too late."

When I awoke, I was sweating, crying, repenting for my sins, and begging God not to leave me behind. I called Nanny to tell her about my dream.

She said, "Meka I keep telling you that you've been called and chosen. Stop running from the Lord and surrender to His will. He wants to use you."

My second most vivid dream about God was when I dreamt I was in a holiness church. I was sitting in the very back pew and hearing a newborn baby's cry. People were speaking in tongues, praising, and worshipping and nobody was paying the baby any attention. I seem to have been the only one who could hear the baby's cry getting louder and louder. I looked around the church to see if I could see the baby, but I couldn't. Then, I looked out into the aisle, and upfront, at the right of the alter, was a baby carrier. It was turned away from the congregation.

I got up, walked up front toward the baby carrier, and looked down at the baby. The baby looked up at me and started speaking in tongues. I looked around the church to see if anybody else was seeing and hearing it. Nobody could see it except me.

I was pointing and saying, "Look, look, look at the baby!!"

Yet, nobody ever responded, and I woke up. Again, I called my nanny for her interpretation.

She said, "Meka that baby was you. God's telling you to come to Him humble as a little child and He will make you a mighty woman of God for His Kingdom."

I've always had a spiritual connection to the Lord, and I held onto that connection throughout my life, especially as I got older. It was my faith and what I'd already come to know about Him early on that helped me through my adversities as an adult.

There have been many other times and encounters with God throughout my life that you'll read about on the following pages.

A Daughter's Broken Heart

CHAPTER 3

My dad was an upcoming boxer who fought around town at the community recreational centers and for Golden Gloves. He had big dreams of one day becoming the heavyweight champion of the world. Most of the older people from the community where I grew up knew or heard of my dad because of his amateur fighting career and because he had a way with the ladies. I remember when his friends would call me little Tommy whenever they'd see me outside somewhere and how proud it made me feel.

When I was a first grader attending Eastport Elementary School, my father showed up one day with a dozen roses for me. I had never seen any of the other little girl's dad do that for them, so I felt special and extremely proud. When he walked into my classroom, I remember how he swooped me up in his arms. He told me he was coming to my grandmother's later that evening to pick me up take me with him. After school, I ran home with excitement. The school was directly across from my grandmother's house.

She dressed me in a white, pink, and black polka dot dress. I remember thinking how pretty I looked and could not wait for my daddy to see me. I went outside to wait for him on the front porch. I watched every car that drove up or down that street. I waited on him for hours. My grandmother walked back and forth to the front door to check on me. As time passed, the sun began to set. I could hear Mama (Grandmother) say, "Come on in here, baby, he's not coming."

Oh, the heartache and disappointment I felt. I realized what she was saying was true. He, in fact, wasn't coming. That began the many times my father would make and break promises to come see and spend time with me. Over the course of my childhood and teenage years, this was my relationship with my dad. He'd pop up or call out of the blue to tell me he was coming. I'd be just as excited to hear from him each time, and each time I'd end up disappointed.

As I got older, my mother told me the story of how my daddy came to the hospital when I was first born, but after visiting for a minute, he went downstairs for cigarettes and never returned. This has always been a habit of his, and it continued throughout my childhood, teen years, and adult life until he passed. Somehow, none of that mattered to me. I still loved that man very much. In my eyes, he couldn't do anything wrong. He was my daddy. He was handsome, strong, and I loved him with all my heart.

My next big experience with my dad came one summer when he took me back to his home state of Georgia for Summer break. I was meeting his side of the family. It would be my first time ever meeting my grandparents, aunts, uncles, siblings, and cousins.

> This has always been a habit of his, and it continued throughout my childhood, teen years, and adult life until he passed.

When we arrived and after I was introduced to everyone, I went to spend the night with my dad's sister. I ended up staying the duration of my summer visit at her house, hardly seeing my dad at all.

Summer had come to an end, and it was time for my dad to take me back to Knoxville. It was the first and last time I'd ever get to see my paternal grandparents. The next time I saw them I was an adult. A couple of years passed, and my dad returned to Knoxville to see me again. As usual, I was ecstatic. My best friend (at the time) and I were outside when my dad arrived. I introduced her to him. Her parents were married, still together, and living in the same household. At times, I secretly wondered what it was like having both parents in your life and being raised by them together.

After staying for about an hour, my dad asked us if we'd like for him to take us somewhere to do something fun. We were excited. After agreeing, we said we'd like to go to the skating rink. He told us to get ready, and he'd be back in a couple of hours to pick us up. Then, he left. With excitement we ran to her parents' house to ask their permission if she could go. They agreed. I was so excited about that moment for different reasons than my friend. For once, it was my dad taking us somewhere. He was paying for it, and it felt good that my best friend was able to see I had a daddy in my life too.

We returned to my house to wait on my dad only for him to not show up. While waiting, I prayed and hoped secretly he wouldn't break his promise like all those other times.

I thought, *Surely he'll come because he seemed so convincing and more sincere than before.*

When he didn't show up, we were both disappointed and sad that he didn't come back to take us where he'd promised just a couple of hours before. The intensity of those emotions for me were more intense than the other times because he didn't just lie to me. He lied to me in front of my best friend, and he lied to her too. I began to cry, and my best friend put her arm around my shoulders and said, "Don't cry. Let's just go to my house."

She tried to comfort me to the best of her ability. Having her there at that moment did help me feel better, but I never forgot. I remained angry with my dad for a very long time after that day. Of course, another long period of not seeing him followed.

A couple of weeks had passed. Then, another friend of mine who lived in the neighborhood came to my house. What she said shocked me. She told me she met my little brother. He rode the same school bus we did, and he wanted to meet me. I thought surely there must be some mistake. *I don't have any paternal siblings here in Knoxville.* The only brother I knew on my dad's side lived in Georgia. She said, "I'll bring him by tomorrow."

The next day came, and she returned to introduce this tall, very handsome, brown skinned boy who was the absolute spitting image of my dad. He also had the same name as my dad. I recognized him from the bus. We never knew we were brother and sister. I couldn't believe it, and it was one of the best things that happened to me thus far. I was proud to know I had another little brother right there in town. We bonded instantly. From that day, my little brother became my big brother in his mind. We were only a couple of years a part, yet we never knew each other existed until that day. How could Daddy have two kids who lived in the same city and state, not too far from one another, and weren't that far apart in age? I couldn't and didn't remember him ever telling me something of that importance! I later discovered I had more siblings Daddy fathered. They also lived in Knoxville, two other brothers and a sister.

As years passed, I was able to meet them all, build relationships with them, and grew to love them all for different reasons!! I think I bonded more with the boys because they looked so much like our daddy, and I could see him every time I looked at them.

There were several more visits from Dad and more broken promises until I got the final out of the blue phone call from him telling me he was coming to town. By that time, I was grown with three children of my own. We talked for an unusual long period of time, and I had the opportunity to express my disappointment in him for missing out on so many important things in my life, but none of it ever took away the love I felt for him. He apologized for not being there for me as he should've been and how much he always loved me. It was a beautiful yet therapeutic phone call. I was able to get a lot of things off my chest I hadn't been able to in the past. Before hanging up, I made him promise to keep his word about coming to Knoxville to see me and meet his grandchildren. He promised. Then, he followed up by saying, "Nothing but death could keep me from it."

A couple weeks later, I received a phone call from my little brother T.C, telling me our dad had a heart attack and died. I was crushed! I couldn't believe it. I wasn't going to hear my daddy's voice anymore or get anymore pop-up visits. It was over. He was gone forever.

I traveled to Georgia for my father's funeral, and I was able to say my goodbyes. I kissed him on his forehead as he lay there in his casket. I told him I loved him. That day, we buried my father. During Daddy's funeral, I was able to see my other older siblings who I hadn't seen since I was a kid during one summer break, and I was able to meet a few more younger siblings. The memories I had were all his broken promises. He lived on in my memory and heart.

Through therapy later in life, I came to realize that experience with my father was a part of why I chose to date certain men. Dysfunction didn't seem like dysfunction at all. I was searching for things in those men I never got from my dad.

> I was searching for things in those men I never got from my dad.

I needed someone to love me, provide for me, protect me, fight for me, and lead me as a man should.

After his burial, I left Georgia with a broken heart and returned to Knoxville. During the ride home, I remember thinking how I never heard my father say he was sorry for not being there for me. There were so many things left unsaid between the two of us. There were so many things he never knew about me nor did I about him. I never got the chance to tell him about all the abuse I suffered at the hands of other men throughout my life and how I never, not even for a moment, blamed him nor hated him for any of it. I simply wanted to know why he wasn't there. He died before I ever got the chance to tell or ask him, and his passing left me with a void, feeling cheated, and abandoned all over again.

My dad fathered several children, 11 that I know of for certain, and there has been talk of there being more. Of the 11 children he fathered, five of us are from Knoxville. I've had the pleasure of meeting and getting to know and love them. In getting to know them, I discovered we all share a couple of things in common. We all look very much like him, and we all had similar experiences with him.

Stolen Innocence

CHAPTER 4

As a kid, the summer was my favorite time of year. School would be out for summer break, and this meant we could stay outside and play a little later than we could during the school year.

Back then, we had to be a little more creative when it came to finding things to occupy our time or entertain ourselves. Kids today have iPhones, laptops, gaming systems, and more. Coming up, just having your own kiddie pool in the front or backyard was a big thing in my neighborhood.

One time, my cousin Rochelle and I decided (without permission) to go to her house to swim in her kiddie pool. We couldn't have been more than six and eight years old with Rochelle being the oldest. We were innocent children just wanting to have fun. We didn't know anything about and child abuse or sexual predators, so we made the decision to take off all our clothes in broad daylight to go for a swim.

My cousin's apartment building faced one of the main roads, and everyone who passed by could see us outside butt naked swimming in the pool. Someone went and told her mom, and we got a whipping. I'll never forget it, and needless to say, we never skinny dipped again.

As grown women now, we often reminisce about that day, and we still get tickled. We often ask, "Whose idea was it?" We blame each other, laugh, and say, "Those were the good ole days." Aside from swimming, we used egg cartons to play marbles, rocks from the ground to play jack rocks, and old broken clothes lines to jump rope. My favorite thing of all was to get old mason jars, chase down, and capture lightening bugs. The boys would fly their kites, and the girls would play hopscotch on the sidewalks.

> I'll never forget it, and needless to say, we never skinny dipped again.

We also had a recreational center in our community where we would go during the day. They provided breakfast and lunch, along with plenty of activities and field trips to different places.

We were like one big family in Mechanicsville. It was a tight knit community. Everyone knew each other or were related in some way. Our parents would hang out, visit each other's home, or go out and party together. Just like most kids, we'd play good together one day and fight the next.

I was that kid that would always run home. I'd bust down Grandma's back door running away from neighborhood girls my age who wanted to jump me for whatever reasons. That is until the day I snatched that back screen door open, and Grandma was standing right there. She took her hand, pushed me right back out of the door, shut the screen, and locked it.

I knew what that meant without her having to tell me. I had to stop running and fight back. It was either fight back or get in trouble with her, so I won that fight that day. Winning that fight did something for my confidence. After that day, win, lose, or draw, I never ran again. It wasn't funny then, but it's hilarious now. Thank you, Grandma.

Most of the people that lived in that community had generational ties to it. Ms. Evelyn was one of those longstanding residents of the neighborhood, and she was the neighborhood babysitter.

On the weekends, she kept everybody's children and grandkids for a couple of quarts of beer while they went out or had to work nights. Despite her drinking, Ms. Evelyn took great care of us. She made sure we were safe, fed, had baths, and were in bed at a decent hour. Then, she'd go sit on her front porch and enjoy her beer. The next morning she'd already be up and have breakfast ready for us before we were picked up by our parents.

Then, there was Ms. Lucius. She was a good friend of my grandmother's. She was another longstanding member of the community. Ms. Lucius lived three doors down from my granny.

She had the prettiest flower garden I ever did see. I was drawn to it. Every day, I would sneak in her flower garden and pick a few flowers, not knowing it was hurting her garden.

On a couple of occasions, she asked me not to pick her flowers, but being hard-headed, I did it anyway. Then, one day she was standing in her kitchen window, and I didn't see her. I tiptoed to the garden, and just as I got ready to pluck the flowers, she opened her door. I didn't know whether to run or fake passing out. I was caught red-handed. I knew she was going to tell my grandmother, and I'd be in trouble for sure, but she didn't.

Instead, she said "Dump, I asked you not to pluck my flowers."

I put my head down and said, "Yes, ma'am, I'm sorry."

Instead of her scolding me or telling on me, she propositioned me. If I promised to stop plucking her flowers, she'd give me candy. At that moment, I learned a way to get free candy every day.

Each day following that incident, I went to her house after school. I pretended as I was going to pluck her flowers, so she'd come on out with that candy to pay me off. It became our little daily ritual. Ms. Lucius would be standing in that kitchen window waiting for me to walk up. Looking back on it now, I believe she enjoyed that little ritual just as much as I did.

Just as much as I was curious and playful, at times I was extremely hardheaded, rambunctious, and rough like a little boy. Out of my mother's three children (two boys and one girl), I was the one to break my arm on my brother's skateboard, the one who got hit by a car after sneaking out of my grandmother's back door, and the one who had to have stiches put in my leg from a bike accident.

My poor mother stayed in the emergency room with me, which brings me to a time when the hospital was trying to get me to say that my mother had physically abused me. That wasn't the case of course. I had been playing rodeo with my older brother and my cousin Buster. I was the bull and came charging at them headfirst. They stepped out of the way, and I hit a concrete wall face first at full speed. It caused a concussion, two black eyes, and a knot on my forehead the size of a golf ball. I definitely looked as if I had been beaten, so my story of what had actually happened wasn't believable. They were convinced I had been abused and was afraid to tell.

After a while of questioning me and me refusing to admit I had been abused, they finally released me to my mother. I had never been abused and really didn't know what it was, but I soon found out.

It was a day like any other. School was out, and I was in the courtyard playing when my name was called by a grown woman. My family and I knew her, and I trusted her because she was a longstanding member of that community as well.

> She proceeded to remove the lower part of my clothing and lay me on the bed.

She called out to me, "Tameka, come here."

I went to see what she wanted. She opened her screen door and told me to come inside. When I got inside, she and her then boyfriend took me upstairs and into her bedroom. She also called out for her nephew to come upstairs.

When he got there, she proceeded to remove the lower part of my clothing and lay me on the bed. Her boyfriend told her nephew to get on top of me. He did as he was told, and I felt a sharp piercing pain. They placed his penis inside of me. It didn't last long because I began to cry, and I think they got scared. They proceeded to tell me I had done something wrong. If I told, I would get in trouble.

I was so afraid I peed on myself because I didn't want to get into trouble. However, I never forgot a single second of that traumatic ordeal, and I never told a soul until I was in my 30's.

Before reading any further, statistics show that 96% of the people who abuse children are male. The younger the victim the more likely the abuser is a family member. In addition, 1 in 8 Black children are molested. In "the Black community," mental illness and child sexual abuse are taboo. Those are not conversations you have loud around the dinner table or at family functions.

I know my mom and grandmother would have protected me with their lives, but I don't think either one of them thought for one minute that someone in our own family was capable of any of this. I truly believe they thought it would more likely be a complete stranger they had to watch out for and protect me from. That wasn't the case. I don't want to hurt anyone or make anyone look bad. My intentions are purely to educate and empower through my story.

When I was around six or seven-years-old, I was downstairs watching T.V., and my grandmother was out on the front porch when a relative told me to come upstairs. I can't remember exactly if he was an uncle or cousin. That part I blocked out of my mind. When I got upstairs, he took me into a bedroom, laid me on my stomach, and pulled my clothes and panties down. As he attempted to carry out his assault on me, my grandmother burst into the door.

She immediately yelled, "Get up off of that damn baby!!!!!!" I began to cry.

I was not sure if he was going to sodomize me or what. All I know is my grandmother saved me! She grabbed me up off the bed, pulled my clothes back up, and put her arms around me. I don't remember anything else that happened beyond that point and I'm glad. I don't want to remember anything more than what I do remember. I guess it's my mind's way of protecting itself.

Unfortunately, my mama and grandmother couldn't protect me from everyone. I continued to be molested by family members and friends of the family. Although I was a child mentally and emotionally, my body was growing ahead of its time. I believe this is what attracted the abusers to me. I was physically developed, yet I still had a childlike mind. That made me easy prey, and they knew it.

One of my abusers molested me every chance he got until I was around 11 or 12. It stopped when I was old enough to really know and understand that what was being done to me was wrong, and I was a little more likely to expose him and his sickening deeds.

I've had abusers to ejaculate on me, have me play with them, and who'd fondle me on several occasions. I was ashamed and truly felt that it was me. I felt I was the one doing wrong, and I didn't want to get in trouble. I believed they'd eventually stop, but the mental and emotional damage had already been done. Yet, I remained silent and carried those dark secrets for years.

When the summer of 86' rolled around, I was turning 12 in December, and I was going to stay with my grandmother for the summer. By that time, she had gotten remarried and moved to Chattanooga, Tennessee. I was so excited and ready to see her. I missed her dearly and couldn't wait to spend the summer with her. When I got to Chattanooga, my life changed forever. Let me remind you. By this time, I was fully developed. I didn't have a typical 12-year old's body frame. My breast had filled in and so had my hips, thighs, and butt. One could tell by my babyface and by talking to me that I was still a minor. However, my body was built like that of a woman's.

I was walking to a local convenience store, which was only a couple of blocks from where my grandmother lived. I passed this guy. For privacy reasons, I will call him Raymond. He was outside washing his Monte Carlo with his music blaring. As I walked another block, I could hear the blaring music coming up behind me. He pulled up beside me and asked where I was going and if I wanted a ride? Initially, I said no. After all, I had been taught not to take rides from strangers.

Oh, but he was persistent, and he was handsome. I still didn't get in the car with him that day. For the next few days, I took a trip to the store just to see if he'd be outside. Sure enough, he was there. Around about the fourth time, he called me over to him. Me being the gullible, naive, hardheaded preteen, I bit the bait.

He finessed me and convinced me I was safe with him. After a couple of weeks of this, he talked me into coming into his house where he got me to feel even more comfortable with him. I let my guard down some more, and he became the first man to have sex with me. He didn't force me to have sex. I was a participant. However, legally a minor can't consent to having sex.

As weeks passed, I continued to sneak away, and he'd meet me at designated spots to pick me up in his car. Eventually I was caught by my step grandfather's nephew. I was getting into this man's car, and my family member informed my grandmother. She grounded me and insisted that I stop seeing him. She even threatened to send me back home to my mother before the summer was over.

I would sneak and call him, and he would try to convince me to get away so we could see each other. My grandmother guarded me so much that sneaking away was almost impossible until one day she had to work later than usual. My grandfather had gone fishing with his friends, so I snuck away. Raymond only lived a couple of blocks away from my grandparents, so I thought I could see him and make it back in time before either of them returned home.

Without calling him, I decided to surprise him and just show up. When I arrived at his house, his brother and a group of his friends were all on the porch. I asked where I could find Raymond. I was told he wasn't there, but he could take me to him. I wanted to see him and knew I didn't have much time so I agreed. His brother, along with four of his friends, walked me a few blocks away to a house I had never been to before.

Upon arriving, they told me to come in and wait, and he'd be pulling up soon. Me being the naive and unsuspecting child I was went inside with these 5 young men. Once inside, the brother and his friends took turns taking off my clothes, ripping my panties off, and raping me. I cried and begged them to stop and take me home. I told them I was going to get into trouble, and my grandmother would be looking for me. They laughed and continued taking turns.

This lasted quite some time, and I was terribly distraught. Suddenly, I heard a loud knock on the bedroom door. I was hoping it was my boyfriend coming to rescue me. The one on top of me got up and left the room. When he returned, he told me to get dressed, and he had a ride to take me back home.

Still crying, I reached for my clothes and got dressed as quickly as I could. As we approached the living room of the house, I saw two older gentlemen. I think they must've been in their late 20's or early 30's. They told me to come with them, and they would take me home. On the way, I noticed they had passed the road that would take me to my grandmother's. When I spoke up and said something, I was told to shut up and not make a sound.

I remember the extreme sense of regret for sneaking out of the house and the intense fear of not only what was going to happen with those men, but what kind of trouble I'd be in when my grandmother found out. It began to get dark outside, and we pulled into the alley behind a church. The gentleman on the passenger side ordered the driver to pull to the back of the church and cut the car and lights off. He then got out of the passenger seat and into the backseat with me. I knew what was about to happen and began to cry hysterically. He grabbed me by my arm and said, "Don't make me hurt you. Be quiet."

My God, the array of emotions I felt at that moment paralyzed me. I couldn't do anything. I was too afraid. I thought I was going to die. I thought to myself, *There is no turning back now. Once they finish doing whatever they're going to do with me, they're going to kill me.* He then ordered me out of the car and made me take part of my clothing off, and those two older men raped me at the back of that church.

> If I get out of this, how do I tell what happened and what kind of trouble will I be in?

They continued to go back and forth for what seemed like eternity until one became angry because the other was taking too long. They began to argue. The one who was driving got into the car and pulled off. He left us right there in the dark behind the church all alone. He said, "Get dressed and let's go."

We began walking through the alley, and I thought I would be found dead there. I couldn't believe everything that had happened from the time I snuck away from home that day until that moment. I had been raped by seven men. I just couldn't believe how my boyfriend's brother tricked me and participated in all of it. *If I get out of this, how do I tell what happened and what kind of trouble will I be in?* I wondered. I also worried about how my boyfriend would react. Would he break up with me?

My mindset was that of a child's because I was a child. After walking a good distance, he was able to flag down a taxi, and he boldly took me home. I knew my grandparents would be there upset and waiting for me. Rather than bring awareness to what that stranger had just done to me, I was more worried about getting in trouble. I was also afraid of him because he'd participated in gang raping me. I was afraid of him knowing exactly which house I lived in. I thought he'd come back to do it again.

I had them to drop me off a block away from where I lived. When the taxi pulled off, I ran as fast as I could to the house. Of course, my grandmother was sitting in the living room waiting for me, and she was very upset and worried about me, I'm sure. She asked where I had been, yelled at me, and told me she was taking me back to Knoxville that upcoming weekend. I couldn't tell her. I couldn't tell her. I just couldn't tell her!

I went to the bathroom to take a bath. For two hours, I sat in that tub trying to scrub off the filth, lies, and shame of what had just happened to me. I buried my face in a towel and cried my heart out.

The Friday before leaving to go back home, I managed to call my boyfriend to let him know that I was leaving. We both cried, said how much we'd miss each other, and he promised he'd come to Knoxville to see me. I told him my mother would never allow it, so I wouldn't be able to see him if he came. He told me he'd figure out a way and not to worry.

The end of the summer came, and I started back school. There was no contact from Raymond. Then, one day my mother told me not to leave the house because Raymond had come to town. I unknowingly left my contact number book at his house, and he contacted a childhood friend of mine to find out my address. Her mother called my mom, so that's how she found out.

Later on that day Raymond called the house, and I just so happened to answer the phone. He told me where he was and that he wanted to see me. There was no Google maps or GPS back then, yet he was able to get directions from total strangers on how to get to my address. There was a corner store a block from where we lived, and he was calling me from the payphone outside the store. I hurried and packed a bag, snuck out of the house, and ran to the store where he sat waiting for me, but he wasn't alone. He had brought his friend from Chattanooga along with him. I was surprised to see him because Raymond hadn't mentioned it.

It didn't matter for too long because I was running away with the man I was so in love with and whom I thought loved me. Raymond took me to a Hotel that night, but he only paid for one room with double beds. Once inside, I had the chance to tell him what his brother had done to me in Chattanooga. He got angry and began to cry. Then, he began to blame me, as if I was somehow responsible for being gang raped.

After an emotional and heated argument, I went to take a shower. When I came out, Raymond wanted to have sex, but I didn't want to because his friend was there. That was when Raymond said, "If you love me, you will let my friend have sex with you too." I was devastated. Although I was only 12, I knew that was not what someone who truly loves you would want you to do. Raymond made me feel I needed to do it to prove my love for him, so I did, and he sat there emotionless and unbothered. At that moment, I was being taught what love wasn't.

The morning came, and it was checkout time. Raymond told me to get dressed because it was time to go. I assumed he meant hitting the highway to drive us back to Chattanooga. We left the hotel, and instead of him going in the direction of the highway, he was heading in the direction of where I lived. I began to question him and cry. I didn't understand why he'd have me do all those things just to break his promises to me. He told me he couldn't take me back with him because he'd go to jail for kidnapping. I replied, "Well, if I stay, my mom is going to kill me. I can't go back home now. You have to take me with you.

He refused, and I simply fell apart. As we drove and got closer to where I lived, I began to beg him to take me with him. If he took me home, I knew I'd never be able to see him again. My mom would make sure of it. Of course, he didn't listen and took me back to the store where he picked me up the day before.

> I jumped on the hood of the car screaming at the top of my lungs,

As he tried to leave, I jumped on the hood of the car screaming at the top of my lungs, "Please don't go."

That's when my neighbor saw us and called my mom. Moments later, the police and my mom showed up. They took us both to juvenile where we would stay overnight and face a judge the next morning. The following morning, they had me in the court dressed in an all-orange jumpsuit. When they brought him in, he was in all-orange with shackles on his ankles and handcuffs on his wrist. The judge ordered us to stay away from each other and told him he could never contact me or return to Knoxville again. If he did, he would be sent to prison. I never saw nor heard from Raymond anymore until I became an adult.

A few months later, my little brother got sick with the flu. A few days later, I developed similar symptoms. My little brother got better, but my sickness lingered, and the only food (it seemed) I could eat and keep down or even wanted to eat were pickles. I was having a hard time buttoning my pants, and my breast were sore. I noticed I hadn't been getting my period, yet my mom was still buying me menstrual pads, and I was hiding them in my top drawer. During this time, my great aunt Sara would visit my mom's house every day when she got off work. Every day, I was on that couch asleep when she arrived. One day she came by just as I was dozing off. She finally said to my mom, "That child is pregnant." My eyes nearly popped out of their sockets. *Oh my God, is that what's wrong? I thought to myself.*

Later that evening, my mom told me to go take a shower, put on some clean clothes, and get ready. She was taking me to the hospital. When I arrived, I was given one of those hospital gowns and told to undress. As soon as I took off my bra, my mother looked at my breast with extreme concern.

She asked, "How long has those stretch marks been on your breast Tameka?"

I replied, "I don't know."

In walked the doctor. When he instructed me to climb on top of the examination table, he touched me all around my stomach, pressing and mashing in a circular motion.

He finally said, "Without running any laboratory test, I

can tell you exactly what's wrong with her. She's about 16 weeks pregnant...Four months."

My mom looked at me. Her mouth fell open, and she backed up against the wall and began to cry. Oh my God. I hated to hear my mom cry. I still don't. Her crying made me cry. Besides that, I thought she was going to kill me. I was a   12-year-old black girl, in the 6th grade, and pregnant at a time I was attending a predominantly white school. I will never forget the stares from the teachers and students and all the questions I was asked.

Back in the 80's, abortions were treated and handled differently. Because I was so far along in my pregnancy, I couldn't get one. My mom and I had even discussed adoption, but I wanted to keep my son. By the time he was born, my mom was already in love with him and had accepted the fact that he was coming.

Months later, my mom got a phone call from my uncle in Chattanooga. She was told to get there as soon as possible because my grandmother had a stroke. She left immediately to check on Grandma, and I remember the phone ringing hours later and hearing Mama scream, "She's gone!" It felt like my world had come to an end. My beautiful grandmother had passed away. I was devastated and bereaved. She never had the chance to see and meet her very first great grandson.

A few months later, on April 5, 1987, I started having contractions, and my mom took me to the hospital. It was my first pregnancy and delivery. First time deliveries are typically longer and harder. I had been in labor for so long that my mom had decided to go home to get some rest. We didn't live too far from the hospital, so she told the nurses to call her when I started dilating. She wanted to be back in time for me to start pushing.

During my prenatal appointments, I had been given a video to watch about epidurals and the dangers of being paralyzed because of it, so when they offered, I refused it. My refusal to take the epidural must've frustrated the nurse taking care of me because she asked with an angry tone, "Are you in pain or are you just whining?" I believe she was judging me for being a kid in the hospital having a baby, and she was annoyed by all my screaming and crying. Finally, I began to dilate, and my mom returned to the hospital.

She walked in on the nurse trying to insist that I take the epidural. Mama spoke up, "She said she didn't want it. Leave her alone!" After hours of labor, I gave birth to my first child, a baby boy. My mama named him Jarret LaBee' Smith. Jarret was a beautiful little chocolate baby boy with a head full of hair. He was and still is one of the greatest gifts ever given to me. We were mother and son, but because of my age, I was still a child myself, and we were both being raised by my mom.

I was a teenage mom, but I knew nothing about being a mother. I had the physical responsibilities of feeding, bathing, dressing, and putting my baby to sleep all while maintaining my schoolwork and grades. My mom was the one with the financial responsibility of providing for and raising us. I thank God I had and still have her for a mother and a grandmother for my kids because she did an awesome job raising her own children and helping to raise her grandchildren and great grandchildren.

My mom did the very best she could with what she had, and I'm forever grateful to God for her!

Searching For Love in all the Wrong Places

CHAPTER 5

As a growing teenage girl, I became even more rebellious and defiant. I was sneaking and wearing makeup after my mom absolutely forbid it. I hung out with other females older than me, skipped school, and was attracted and drawn to older males, which led to promiscuity.

This takes me to whom I'll call Avery. He was in high school, and I was a 7th grader. Avery showed interest in me, and I became fully involved in a relationship with him that was very sexual. As the relationship continued, I started getting into more trouble. I had failing grades, was fighting and missing school, and things of that nature. I became totally unfocused and out of control.

Eventually, my mom found out about Avery, and I was forbidden to see or have any further contact with him. Soon, I started sneaking him into the house through my bedroom window while my mom was asleep. I got away with it for quite some time until one night Avery knocked over a fan. It hit the floor, making a very loud noise, which woke my mom. We heard her coming to checkout where the noise came from, and Avery immediately hid in my bedroom closet and stayed there for at least 45 minutes until we both thought she'd gone back to sleep. When the coast was clear, he escaped through the window.

> Avery couldn't leave through the door, climb out of the window, or…

One evening, my mom and her then boyfriend went to the grocery store. I called Avery to come over. He only lived a few houses up the road. We thought we had time to sneak and see each other before they returned, but we lost track of time. We didn't hear them pull up, so we had no time to respond and avoid being caught. Avery couldn't leave through the door, climb out of the window, or even hide in my closet. The only thing left to do was for him to hide behind my bedroom door. I shut off the lights and ran into the living room as if nothing was wrong. I guess my mom's boyfriend could tell I was startled and acting nervously, so he walked through the house and then all hell broke loose.

I heard a scuffle and loud voices coming from the hallway right outside of my bedroom. My mom's boyfriend found Avery in my room hiding behind the door, and he tried to get away. He yelled for my mom, and it was *on and popping* from there. Her boyfriend yelled, "Break his damn back, Rose." After an intense wrestling match between Avery and Mom's boyfriend me screaming and crying, and my mom tussling with me, it had gotten totally out of hand. I was trying to protect Avery and shoved my mom. I never intended for that to happen, which I regret, even until this day. However, I was a naive and extremely gullible child who thought she was in love again.

At this point, my mom dared me to see him or for him to even come within five feet of me ever again. She threatened to press charges and do whatever necessary legally to keep him away from me. Yet, I was absolutely determined to continue seeing and having a relationship with him one way or another, so I became even more defiant. I continued sneaking to call and see him. We got so desperate to see each other, so one day he drove to the middle school I attended, and I skipped class to meet him near the back exit of the school. Avery hit a teacher's parked car, and the police were called. That cut out the school visits and me cutting class. He was prohibited from being on the school's grounds ever again. That still didn't deter us from seeing each other.

One weekend, my mom decided to cut me some slack and give me a break from the baby. I was allowed to spend the night with a female cousin. Her mom was a little less strict and worked nights. Still defiant and hardheaded, I was able to call Avery and talk on the phone with him. It just so happened that he too had a cousin visiting him for the weekend, and he wanted to meet my cousin. They told us about a house party they were headed to. My cousin and I decided to sneak away and go as well. My mom would have never allowed me to go to any house party.

I was excited and couldn't wait to go because I had never been to a house party before. Besides that, it had been a minute since I last saw Avery, and he was going to meet me there. Some kind of way, my mom found out about the party and that I wasn't at my cousin's house. She came looking for me. I remember the kids at the party coming to find me amongst the crowd to warn me that my mom was outside looking for me. I took off out the backdoor and hid in the woods located behind the house.

When she finally left, Avery came out of the house and called for me to tell me she was gone. He and I left the party alone and went to his uncle's house in a housing project nearby. At this point, it was extremely late, and I was at the point of no return. I knew it would be the end of Avery and I if I went home, so I didn't. One night turned into two, four, and so on. I hadn't been home nor called my mom to even let her know that I was okay. I was officially a first time runaway.

Avery had a job, and he'd go to work during the day and leave me at his uncle's house until he got off. I was living in this carefree fantasy land with the man I loved and no one to tell me what to do. Then, one day as Avery was leaving for work, he spotted my mom, her boyfriend, and the police going into the rental office of the housing complex we were hiding in. He came back immediately to tell me. Just as he did, they were pulling up in the front of the building with the office manager. We knew that meant they had a warrant for me, and they were coming in to get me with or without his uncle's permission.

His uncle's apartment was located on the upper level, so I couldn't go out the front door without being seen and caught, Avery stayed behind. Besides, they were looking for me and not him. As long as he wasn't caught in my presence, he was alright. I climbed out of a back window, jumped down onto the roof of the apartment below, jumped to the ground, and made my escape.

I thought I had gotten away. I ran to a friend's house, but someone spotted me and led my mom and the police right to my location. They surrounded my friend's apartment building. There was nowhere for me to run. I attempted to go out of an upstairs window, but the police were standing there looking right up at me. I was trapped and could hear the police coming up the stairs to detain me. I began crying and begging my mom to not send me to juvenile. It didn't help. She was tired and had done everything she could to protect and get me to obey her. She had no other choice but to lock me up to protect me from me.

> I climbed out of a back window, jumped down onto the roof of the apartment below, jumped to the ground, and made my escape.

I began threatening suicide and quickly learned that wouldn't work either. I was taken to juvenile that night, spent a couple of days there, and went to court. Because of my suicide threat, the judge court ordered me to have a psych evaluation at a mental hospital before being sent off to a long-term wilderness camp for troubled teens, indefinitely. I thought my world had come to an end, and it was definitely the end of Avery and me.

For 11 months, I was away at camp. I received plenty of counseling, behavioral health, and I learned a lot of different skills I otherwise wouldn't have. Those skills included building cabins, laying floors, playing volleyball, learning to canoe, white water rafting, mountain climb, and more. I even started listening to and appreciating other music genres and cultures. I was the only black girl in that program for almost a year, so I had a chance to experience things outside of my norm. I picked up a lot of things from them that weren't common where I was from, like head banging and listening to groups such as Gun's and Roses and Whitesnake.

According to the doctors and counselors, I had been reformed and was ready to go home. I graduated from the program and returned home to my family. My son was walking and talking by this time, and we were able to bond even more. I started doing better at home, at school, and my grade got better. I stopped running away from home and hadn't gotten in anymore legal trouble. Then, I went on to start my freshman year of high school. It wasn't long before I started reverting to old patterns and behavior.

That's when I met Mark. He was more of my oldest brother's age. We started secretly seeing each other. I found myself involved sexually with him. I can't remember exactly how we even started seeing each other. I do remember we only saw each other for a couple of months. That was a short-lived experience. One night after having sex with Mark, I went home to shower, ate dinner, and went to bed early because my stomach started hurting. In the middle of the night, I awakened to excruciating abdominal pain, and my bed was absolutely soaked in fresh blood. I thought I was having my period, so I went to the bathroom to prepare to take a shower.

As I undressed, I passed a massive blood clot the size of my fist and began calling for my mom. She called 911 and was instructed to take me to the ER. Upon arrival at the emergency room, we learned I had a miscarriage. The next day I called Mark to tell him. Soon after that, we stopped communicating altogether.

A few months later, I began my sophomore year of high school. I met William. He was around my age, but our relationship was toxic and unhealthy from the start. We first met in home economics class, and we absolutely hated each other. We would often argue in class. I thought he was arrogant and obnoxious. He thought he was God's gift to the ladies. Yes, he was very handsome, and the boy could sing his butt off. All the girls were crazy about him, except me. Nope. I refused to feed that oversized ego of his.

At least that's how I wanted to make him feel. His ego was too big, and he needed to be brought down a notch. He said my mouth was too slick, and I was stuck up. We went at it every day. He'd come in and see me, and just burst out singing to get my attention and annoy me. I'd yell, "Shut up. Some of us really come here to learn, William." That was our flirting phase.

I believe we both knew we really liked each other but enjoyed getting under one another's skin. This toxicity somehow developed into a relationship, and before long, again I found myself in love. We were no longer arch enemies. William and I were now a couple, and everyone knew it.

School continued as usual, but I had been having a problem with another female student since the beginning of the school year. She didn't like me for whatever reason, and she began her quest to start a fight with me. I told my mom about it, and my mom called the school to report it but to no avail. Nothing was done to stop it.

This girl was older, in a higher grade, and had a reputation for fighting. I wasn't scared of her and had already made it up in my mind that I wasn't going to let her hurt me, so I started carrying a box opener to school. One morning on our way to class, I ran into the girl in the hallway. We exchanged words, and she told me she was coming for me after school. Her brother and I were classmates and friends. I went to him and told him I didn't want any trouble with his sister since we were cool, but she kept threatening me. He said he would talk to her in an attempt to deescalate the problem. It didn't work. After school, sure enough she came for me, and we fought.

That was the first time I'd ever gotten so angry. I blanked out and couldn't control it. The next thing I knew I heard the screams of someone saying, "Oh, my God, she cut her." I had mentally blanked out and cut that girl up badly on school property. At which time, I was put into a restraining hold by our male school principal to stop me from further cutting her. They took her to the emergency room, and I was being held in the school's office behind a locked door until the police and my mom arrived.

I was subsequently expelled from public schools. I ended

up going to an alternative school so I could finish out my sophomore year. The fighting with other females had ceased for a moment but fighting with my boyfriend began. William had a problem with alcohol. When he'd drink, he became aggressive and extremely violent. That was a cocktail for disaster. We both had violent tendencies, and our tempers were out of control. As time went on, the abuse became even more frequent and more violent. As it progressed, I remained silent about it because, although I was afraid of him, I loved him!

One day, we were in the backseat of a mutual friend's car on our way to a football game, and we began arguing. William had been drinking and was becoming verbally and physically aggressive. Just as we got ready to park and get out of the car, William leaned over and bit me on my back as hard as he could. He bit me so hard it broke the skin and left an imprint of his teeth on my back. I jumped out of the car screaming in pain and demanded to be taken home. That was the first time my mom became aware that I was being physically assaulted by him, and she was livid.

When he called later that evening, my mom answered and gave him an ear full. She told him he'd better keep his hands off her child. She wasn't going for it. If we couldn't get along, we needed to leave each other alone.

Along with his love for alcohol and his abuse, William also loved the ladies. I often had run ins with different females about him and found myself fighting or terrorizing someone over him. When I say terrorizing, I mean it. I was horrible when it came to him. Our relationship was the textbook definition of unhealthy and dangerous. We were the epitome of dysfunctional and toxic!

One morning, I awakened to a terrible stomachache. I thought maybe I was pregnant again and having another miscarriage. I was afraid to let Mama know, so the next day I skipped school to go to the local health department to have a test done. Back then, we didn't need our parent present for those things like today.

The pregnancy test came back negative but positive for a sexually transmitted disease. He gave me three STDs. I was terrified, humiliated, and angry all at the same time. I tested positive for gonorrhea, chlamydia, and syphilis but was waiting for the results of my HIV and AIDS test to come back. Back in the early 90's is when Magic Johnson revealed to the world that he had contracted HIV. That became a fear of mine.

I can't remember exactly how Mama found out I had been to the health department, but she confronted me about not talking to her and making her aware of what was going on. She said, "Tameka don't wait until I'm dead and come stand over my grave screaming and hollering because it'll be too late."

Those words pierced my soul, but I still couldn't bring myself to tell her I had contracted not 1 but three STD'S at the same time. TO GOD BE THE GLORY. I WAS TREATED FOR THE THREE STDS, AND MY HIV/AIDS TEST CAME BACK NEGATIVE.

I started back skipping school and staying out all night. I got so far behind that my efforts and focus were no longer on school, and I later dropped out completely. By that point, I was completely out of my mother's control. She couldn't do anything with me. I was rebellious and defiant. Had Mama tried to stop me, I would've only ran.

William and I were still broken up behind the STD situation when I ran into a local, well-known, big-time, drug dealer. He was notorious for being involved with young girls. I was 16, out of control, and the perfect prey for him. He was dressed in his flashy clothes and sparkling jewelry when he invited me to ride with him in his Caddy.

The car was new, and it was beautiful. It had the loud music, rims, and it screamed everything that would draw attention to him. After promising me I could have anything I wanted if I went out with him, I agreed and got in his car. I felt like I was doing something. *Wait until William hears about this. This will surely pay him back, hearing I'm in the big dope man's car,* I thought.

There also sat a clear plate with a white powdery substance I'd soon be introduced to.

Man, I was such an airhead, stupidly gullible, and naïve. The dope man took me to his house. I was impressed at how beautiful it was. There were many cars parked outside. I remember walking in and seeing a pile of money on the floor. There also sat a clear plate with a white powdery substance I'd soon be introduced to. It was cocaine and beside it sat a cut straw. He had apparently been counting money and getting high when he decided to look for some company to join him.

He asked me if I wanted a drink, and I said yes. I didn't want to seem immature. After a drink or two, he lifted the straw, put some cocaine in it, and took a sniff. He refilled the straw again, looked at me, and told me to sniff. I did....16 years old, and I was being introduced to cocaine. I became his new girl. Well, at least one of them anyway. I ended up staying with him for about a month. He took me shopping for clothes, shoes, and would give me wads of cash and keep my hair looking good. We were going places and doing things I'd never done, and I was on top of the world, but this man was possessive and controlling. I sensed he was dangerous too. I was never out of his sight.

One day, I made up an excuse to leave the dope man's presence, and I went looking for William, never to return to the dope man again. Although he had money and drugs, he was too old for me. I didn't have the same feelings for him that I had for William, so I left and left behind everything he purchased. It was a good thing I left because a couple weeks later the dope man was raided by the feds. They confiscated cars, tractor trailers, motorcycles, houses, money, drugs, and more. He ended up doing a lot of time in federal prison. It's true that God watches over babes and fools!

Suicide

CHAPTER 6

William and I got back together and continued in our relationship as usual. It was still dysfunctional, toxic, and abusive.

In February of 1991, I got pregnant with my second child, and I went to live with William and his grandmother who helped raise him. Ms. Barbara was good to me, and she loved herself some William, but she did not play that fighting crap and disrespect in her house. Thinking back on Ms. Barbara, she reminds me of the Madea character who Tyler Perry plays in some of his movies. She was a hard woman, tall, stout, and carried a pistol.

After a couple of fights in her house, I had to go stay with William's mother while he remained with her. I could've gone home to my mother's, but I knew she would never go for us fighting in her home at all. She wouldn't have been as forgiving as me.

November rolled around, and I gave birth to another son. He was William's first child. A month later I turned 17. It was another hard and painful natural child birthing experience. I had no pain medicine whatsoever, and this time I didn't have a baby without his father being present. William was right there to witness every second of it.

After three days, the baby and I were released from the hospital and returned to William's mother's house. That evening, William left to celebrate the birth of his son and did not return until the next day. When I arrived, he was drunk, and I didn't want him holding the baby, so I took the baby downstairs to his mother. Upon returning upstairs, I began questioning him about where he'd been. I had been calling his grandmother's house and knew he had not been there. The more I asked the angrier he got.

Our argument turned volatile, and the fighting began. We fought hard and long too. Nobody could break us up, and it was getting worse. I was hitting him with objects to get him up off me, so it made it worse. William knocked me backwards into a fish aquarium. The back of my head hit the corner of it and split open. I was wearing a brand new, thick, cotton, royal blue housecoat and blood was spewing from my head down the back of it. That made him stop, and he ran out of the house. By the time the ambulance and police got there, he was gone. My housecoat was soaked in blood, and I was badly injured. It looked as if I had been shot or something, and I became hysterical.

Remember, I was only 3 days out of the hospital. I was still sore, bleeding after giving birth, still had vaginal stitches, and was back in the emergency room getting the back of my head stapled back together. Of course, the hospital called my mom. When she got there and saw me, she began to cry. I had blacked eyes, busted lips, and the back of my head was busted open.

The police looked at me and said, "Thank God you aren't my daughter because I'd be going to jail tonight." I was later released from the hospital. My mom wanted me to come back home with the baby, but I still wasn't done with William. Besides, we had a newborn together. I couldn't leave him. I knew he loved me, and it was only because of the alcohol that he went to that extreme. He wouldn't have hurt me if he'd been sober. Those were the excuses my 17-year-old mind were coming up with to justify my reasoning for wanting to stay in that relationship.

> My housecoat was soaked in blood…

Looking back, I had adapted to toxicity and thought abuse was love. It's all I'd ever known. It's all I'd ever gotten from boys or men, sexually, physically, mentally, or verbally. After the staples were removed and the baby and I had our six weeks checkup, we went to stay the weekend with William at his grandmother's. Everything was going well until William decided to leave that Saturday night and not return until Monday. By Monday, I got up, fed the baby, gave him a bath and got dressed. I plugged in my curling iron, took the baby into Ms. Barbara's room so I could shower and get myself together.

As I stepped out of the shower, I heard William's voice. I could tell he had been drinking. When I walked into the room, he was holding the baby. I immediately went to remove my baby from his arms and made a sly remark, "There's no telling where you've been." He went off. I was still holding the baby when he told me to put him down. As soon as I did, he started punching me. I ran into the other room to get away when he attacked me some more. I reached for my curling iron and laid it on his face. I thought it would burn him enough to stop him from beating me, but it only enraged him more.

I could hear Ms. Barbara screaming for us to stop and could hear our baby screaming at top of his lungs too. By this time, William reached for a thick wooden stick and began beating me with it while I was down on the floor. I managed to get up and ran for the baby, thinking he wouldn't continue to beat me. I was wrong. He drew back the stick and got ready to swing it at my head. That's when I heard Ms. Barbara call him by his full name, pointing her gun at him. She yelled, "I love you, but if you hit that girl while she's holding that baby, I'll shoot you dead right here." Then, she cocked her pistol.

He paused, turned to look at her (so did I), and we knew she absolutely meant what she'd just said. It broke her heart to be put in that position. He dropped the stick and ran out the door. She yelled at me and said, "Y'all need to leave each other alone, or somebody is going to get killed." At that moment, I made it up in my mind that I'd had enough, and I was leaving. I called my mom, and she came to pick me and the baby up.

I was 17 with two children, and that qualified me for my first apartment. My mom had full custody of my oldest son, and he lived with her. I had the baby. I applied for my apartment and moved in a one bedroom a month or two later. After months of us being broken up, William moved on and so did I. We had both jumped right into another relationship with different people.

I began seeing an older guy who I'll call New York. He was a hustler and a ladies' man too. He was recently out of a long-term relationship with another woman around his age and had warned me that she may attempt to confront me.

Three months into our relationship, one night we decided to attend a night club and be seen out in public together. While in the club, we separated for a minute and started mingling with our friends. I was ready to go and walked around the club looking for him, but I couldn't find him. I was told by one of his friends that he'd gone outside. I followed behind him and went outside to look for New York. I spotted him in a small group of people.

I walked over to him to let him know I was ready to go, and an older female spoke up and asked "who I was talking to?".

I responded, "I'm talking to New York."

She replied, "Oh, so you're the little young b@#$& that he's been talking to."

She and I began to exchange words. Then, a fight between she and I immediately ensued. Again, because of my temper, I blanked out. Before I knew it, I could hear her screaming, "She's cutting me. " The fight was broken up, and the police showed up on the scene. I was completely unhinged. I was arrested, taken to jail for the first time in my life, and charged with aggravated assault, which (Thank God) was later thrown out of court. Being the woman I am today, I wish I could go back and undo it. New York bonded me out and took me home.

The following morning, he and I discussed what to do with all the weed he had in my house and who to give what to and how much. Basically, we talked about how to handle the business he was leaving behind because he was due to go to court soon and was expecting to serve some prison time for past criminal charges.

He then gave me a 38-caliber pistol for my own protection and showed me how to load and unload it. Then, we went outside to practice shooting it in the air, and he realized something was wrong with the firing pin or hammer. I can't really remember exactly. It's been so long ago. So, he put the pistol in a bag and placed at the back of our bedroom closet. I told him I didn't need it, and I wasn't used to guns anyway, so he didn't need to worry about trying to get me another one.

New York ended up going to serve his time. I talked to him every day and went to visit him at the county jail before he was shipped off to prison. It had been a while since I'd last talked to or even seen William, but I was very much in contact with his mother and grandmother. In fact, I took our son to his mother's house on February 21 to stay through the weekend. That Saturday, February 23, William showed up at my house drunk and said he just wanted to talk to me about our son. I agreed and let him in.

We talked about everything and even entertained the thought of us getting back together. A neighbor of mine knocked on the door and asked to use my telephone, and William pulled out a handgun and started waving and pointing it everywhere. He even pointed it at my neighbor frightening her. I took it from him and removed the bullet. I was shocked because that was the first time I realized he had a gun. The gun looked almost identical to the 38 New York had left me with, but I knew mine was in my bedroom closet.

When I mentioned to William that I had a gun like his, he replied "Oh, I just have 1 bullet. I need one more. Do you have any 38 bullets?"

At the time, I felt in my spirit to tell him no, so I did. I took his gun to my room to put it on the shelf in my closet and threw the bullet behind my headboard. I did all of that because I knew he had been drinking, and I didn't want him to accidentally hurt anybody.

My neighbor left, and I turned on some music. I played "BABY HOLD ON TO ME" by Gerald Lavert, and I had it on repeat. William and I made love to that song, and I agreed to get back with him. He was wearing a gold herringbone necklace that he took off and put around my neck as a symbol of his love. After having sex, he told me he loved me, and he'd be back. He had something to do. He said it was important, and he had to find some more 38 bullets. I figured maybe he'd gotten into it with someone and wanted them for protection because he only had the one bullet.

I didn't question him any further about why there was such an urgency for more bullets. Besides, I had planned on getting him to stay the night and sleep off the liquor, in hopes that it would change his mindset. He walked out my backdoor and returned about an hour later calmer and appeared to have sobered up a little.

He said, "Damn, I couldn't find anybody with any 38 bullets. Go get my stuff I'm getting ready to go."

I headed towards my bedroom, and he followed. My neighbor returned to use the phone again, so I walked back to the living room to let her in. Once I let her inside, I returned to the bedroom where he stood looking at me. I got his gun and told him to help me move the bed because I had thrown the bullet behind my headboard. After retrieving the bullet, I handed it to him and reached for his gun that I had put on my closet shelf.

He then said, "Sit down. I want to tell you something. You know I love you and nobody else will ever love you the way that I do"

I replied, "I love you too, William."

He continued, "We have a beautiful son together, and I want to say Thank you."

I remember thinking, *Why is he being so sentimental and seems so sad?* I just wrote it off as him drinking too much. What happened next changed my life forever. He put the bullet back in the gun, looked at me and said, "I love you." He put the gun in his mouth and pulled the trigger. Nothing happened, and I looked at him anxiously.

I asked, "WHAT ARE YOU DOING, WILLIAM? STOP!"

The second time he spun the chamber, put the gun to the side of his head, pulled the trigger again, and nothing happened. By this time, I had closed my eyes and plugged my ears with my fingers. I begged him to stop playing.

He said, "You better look, or I'm going to do it."

He opened the chamber of the gun, looked inside, and said "THERE IT IS." He closed it back, put it to the side of his again, and pulled the trigger. This time I heard a loud boom, and the echo rang in my ears unlike anything I'd ever heard in my life. I saw blood splatter. He took a couple steps back, leaned up against my closet, and slowly slid down. His eyes closed, and his head slowly rested to one side. I couldn't move. I was paralyzed and in shock. I couldn't process what had just taken place. Then, I snapped out of it and began to scream at the top of my lungs.

> I saw blood splatter.

I ran out of my bedroom towards the living room. All I could see was the back of my neighbor running out of the front door. She, too, was screaming for help. She thought he'd shot me and was not sure if he was coming after her too. By this time, her boyfriend and his brother were coming through my front door.

I screamed, "He shot himself. He shot himself."

Other neighbors were coming from every direction trying to help him and console me, but they wouldn't let me back into my apartment. I became hysterical, broke loose from them, and tried to get inside. They had locked the front door. With all of my strength, I deliberately put my whole right arm through my living room window screaming, "LET ME IN, SO I CAN TALK TO HIM." Glass shattered everywhere!

I ran to a neighbor's house to call 911 and his mother. I was so hysterical that his mom couldn't understand me.

She yelled, "Get off the phone and let me talk to someone about my baby!"

> Then, I saw them turning around and leaving back out. I thought they couldn't find the right apartment, so I ran behind it screaming and hollering for them to stop.

So, I handed the phone to my neighbor, and I could see the ambulance pulling into our driveway. Then, I saw them turning around and leaving back out. I thought they couldn't find the right apartment, so I ran behind it screaming and hollering for them to stop. Back then, paramedics wouldn't respond to anything involving a violent death without the presence of police. I guess it was their way of protecting a potential crime scene.

Finally, the police and paramedics arrived, along with what seemed like hundreds of spectators from all over. I ran towards my back door, but they had my porch sealed off and wouldn't allow anyone accept law enforcement to enter. That's when I began to yell, "Please let me in to just talk to him. He'll hold on if I can just talk to him."

A female police officer approached me and asked, "What was his name?"

I replied, "Why are you using past tense? What do you mean what was his name? Will you please just let me talk to him?"

She then responded, "It's too late!" At the sound of those words, I totally lost it and hit the ground. My legs went numb, my heart dropped, I felt like I couldn't breathe, and my world had turned upside down. It began pouring down rain, and people were trying to console me, but they couldn't.

My mom and other family members finally arrived to support, comfort, and take me away. As I was being lifted off the ground, I saw his mom and some of his family members arrive. They were approaching the apartment. I ran to his mom and reached my arms out to her.

When she turned away from me, one of his family members started yelling at me, "Why didn't you stop him?"

I couldn't say anything. I was stunned. It devastated me and left me in disbelief that any of this was happening. You have to understand. Prior to all of this, I was extremely close to his family. I lived with them and had been with William for a couple of years. They knew me, so they knew I loved him. I would have never allowed anything to hurt him if I could stop it. Finally, my back door opened, and they brought his body out on a stretcher with an all-white sheet covering him.

I will never forget the pain, the sound of the wailing, and the screams I felt and heard coming from my own body. People were hysterical, grieving, and angry that this had happened, and they wanted answers. I was prepared to give them every single detail from the moment he arrived till that the fatal shot. I had nothing to hide, and nobody knew the facts of the events that took place in my bedroom except God, me, and William.

My mom and family knew I had gone into shock, and they took me to my mom's to care for me and support me through that horrible ordeal. After getting to my mom's, I decided I wanted to go be with William's family, not knowing that they were blaming me for his death. My mom said I needed to let everybody and everything calm down first before contacting any of them. My three-month-old son was with them. He had been with them for a couple days, and I wanted to see and hold him.

Mama said, "I know baby, but just give them some time okay?"

Later that night, my oldest brother Cle came back to mama's and said he was going to go clean my bedroom for me. I insisted on going with him. When we arrived, we went in through the back door, and I walked to my bedroom. Everything was just as we, law enforcement, and the paramedics had left it. His blood was still on the wall, the closet door, and the floor. At that moment, I blanked out, went berserk, and started destroying my bedroom.

My brother grabbed me and said, "That's why I didn't want you to come, Tameka. You didn't need to see this." He calmed me down and took me to sit in my living room while he cleaned my entire room for me. He wiped down walls, doors, and mopped the floor because he knew I couldn't. My brother was being a great and loving big brother.

A few days later, I returned home, and all hell began to break loose. I soon discovered I was being blamed for William's suicide. One day, I decided to call William's mother to check on her and my son. One of his aunts answered and cursed me out. She told me his mom didn't want to talk to me. I was shocked and confused that she was saying these things to me. I was clueless as to why. That is when his mother got on the phone and said, "Since you took my son, I'm going to take yours."

I was devastated and tried my best to understand why she was saying those things. I wanted to know what she had been told, but she hung up on me. Later that evening, I went to her house to get my son, but William's family came out like an angry mob. I was threatened and told I could not get my son back. I ended up having to get the police involved.

The police arrived and went to talk with the family. A few minutes later they came out with my baby. They began to explain the circumstances surrounding the situation, the threat of violence, and the confusion about who had legal custody of the baby. They had no choice but to place my baby in protective services until we went before a judge.

I was further devastated, hurt, afraid, and angry. I couldn't believe what was happening and how they could even think for a second that I'd willingly be involved with something so tragic. I later found out about all the lies and rumors surrounding the events of that day, which had been told to his family. People were saying someone else killed him, and I was covering it up. I learned the names of a few of those individuals who still do not know I am aware of what they did.

I ended up writing a 32-page letter, front and back, explaining to his mother every detail of that tragic evening. I did that in hopes that she'd remember the girl who once lived with her, had been a longtime girlfriend of her son's, and who had given birth to her first grandchild. She knew me better than that, and she should have known I could never be involved with something like that.

My baby ended up with a severe ear infection and needed tubes in his ears. I went to the hospital to visit with him, and William's mother showed up too. I gave her the letter and pleaded with her to read it. A few days later, we attended court and full custody was returned to me. My baby was released from the hospital into my care.

A day before William's funeral, I was getting prepared to go to the service when I heard a knock at the door. I opened it to find a local well-known pastor standing there. He wanted to come in to talk with me. He asked was I going to the funeral. I said, yes. He then said, "Baby, don't go to that funeral. The family is grieving badly, and emotions are high. They're not thinking clearly, and people have put the blame on you. I'd hate for you to go, and something happens to you. Just go say your goodbyes in private and allow the family to grieve together."

I respectfully did as he suggested because I didn't want to turn his funeral service into something ugly. I didn't want to subject the baby to that either. So, I went to the funeral home to say my goodbyes privately. I wanted to see and talk to William one last time. I was able to get one of the programs for his funeral and was shocked and angered to see that my name wasn't even mentioned. I had been with him for a few years and had given birth to his first and only child. These people didn't even mention me, yet they mentioned a girl he hadn't been dating long at all.

After the funeral had come and gone, I received calls and

visits. I heard from mutual friends of ours and some of his cousins as well. I was surprised by their shocking confessions of the days and weeks leading up to February 23. William had been talking about killing me and taking his own life, but each one of them thought he was just talking. They assumed he and I would end up getting back together and everything would calm down and blow over. I couldn't believe what I was hearing.

Months later, I had the opportunity to speak to the girl he had been dating, and she told me he had been at her house a night or two prior to him killing himself, and he had been playing with that same gun. I was so angry that none of these people spoke up about any of this when the rumors, lies, and doubts about what took place were being spread. I remember thinking, *They could've spared me the agony of being blamed for his death. Their knowledge could've put the rumors and lies to rest earlier on.* ***more than that, had they said something sooner, maybe his suicide could've been prevented!*** But it was too late. The damage had been done, and he was gone forever.

One day William's mother called to talk to me. She was calm, soft spoken, and clearly still very much grieving the death of her child. I loved her and was happy to be talking to her without the anger, blaming, and arguing. She asked me if I would allow her the opportunity to raise the baby, to give her a chance to do with him what she didn't get to do with William. I agreed...I granted her that request. The next day she came to get the baby, and he went to live with her. I soon realized that the anger and blaming me was still there when I got summoned to juvenile court. I was in a custody battle for my son.

During our court battle, I had been accused of being an unfit mother and putting the baby at risk because of my poor mothering. The judge ended up granting his paternal grandmother full custody of my baby. None of what had been said about me during the court proceedings was true, but I was still deeply mourning and was dealing with the psychological effects of his father's suicide, so I didn't fight. I didn't fight it because I knew it was going to be hard for me to be what I needed to be for him. He was a constant reminder of everything I had just gone through. He looked so much like his dad, and it felt I was reliving those moments over and over each time I looked at him or even said his name. I was hardly 18 then, and I had witnessed an extremely traumatic event that I knew had changed me mentally and emotionally. I loved my son with everything in me, and that is why I made the decision not to fight. I felt he was better off with them.

> I was hardly 18 then, and I had witnessed an extremely traumatic event that I knew had changed me mentally and emotionally.

After he went to live with his grandmother, I called to check on him, but there was no answer or returned calls. I tried visiting him but was threatened with physical harm. I sent money, bought Christmas and birthday gifts, but later found out from my son that he never knew any of that. Fast forward a couple of years, one day my mom told me Ms. Barbara, William's grandmother, wanted her to bring me by her house to see her. I couldn't believe it, and I was nervous. I had not seen her nor spoken with her in years.

My mom took me to see her. When I got there, I couldn't believe what Ms. Barbara said to me next. She told me she didn't believe I had anything to do with William's death, and she apologized. She said she always thought William reminded her of his uncle. He had committed suicide as well years ago. She apologized again for blaming me. She said she knew it back when everything happened, but she couldn't bring herself to admit or say it out loud. Not too much longer after that, Ms. Barbara passed away. I truly believe that requested visit was her making things right before she passed, and I never mentioned or talked about that visit to anyone until now. I do remember thinking, *Had you spoken up, the family would've listened to you. Had they heard this come from you, they wouldn't have blamed me.* I hated her for it at that moment!

It took me years to heal, forgive, and move on from the tragic events and aftermath of February 23, 1991. I carried a lot of resentment for William committing suicide and for those he'd told of his plans days or weeks prior. I was angry at him for leaving me here to explain it all myself to his family, friends, and more importantly to our son. I admit I never thought of myself as a good mother. I wasn't there for my son like I should've been, and I wish I had been. I didn't fight hard enough to keep him. Therefore, my child grew up hearing the awful lies about his mom, concerning his dad, as well as being unaware of my efforts to be a part of his life.

He's a grown man now. At least 1000 times, he and I have had conversations about the events of that day. Every time, he'd ask the same questions, and I'd give him the same exact answers.

He once said, "Mama, I believe you. I've asked you to tell me what happened that day so many times and not once has your story changed, not one detail."

I replied, "Because the truth never changes."

There's no way I could have remembered to tell the exact events minute by minute without forgetting important details or without adding something.

He said, "I love you, Mama, and I love my other mama (granny) because she raised me. I don't think you're lying, and I don't think my granny is lying either. She just believes the version of the story that makes more sense to her."

At that moment, I understood what he meant, and it

helped me to understand his grandmother even more and why she chose to believe what she did for all those years. No mother would ever want to believe that their child would take their own life regardless of the reason(s). That was simply her way of coping with his death. It took years for me to understand, accept, and find forgiveness for her and everyone who blamed me for his death.

Sadly, William's mother passed away a couple of years ago, but I thank God she and I had the opportunity to make peace with one another. I had the opportunity to tell her thank you for raising and taking good care of my son. We were able to express the love we still felt for one another and would often reminisce about old times. I'm sure she'd be proud to see that my son is now a grown man with a son of his own. I will forever and always hold those good memories in my heart!

More Dysfunctional and Toxic Relationships

CHAPTER 7

The housing project I lived in when William committed suicide allowed me an emergency move transfer, so I chose to go back to where I was more familiar, accepted, and where I felt safe, Mechanicsville. I was 18 with two kids, both of whom were being raised by their grandmother's, which left me with no real responsibilities and only having to care for myself.

Eventually, I met Marcus at a house party. We were from the same side of town and he was just a few years older than me. Marcus was well known on that side of town and had been a high school basketball star, very popular with the ladies, well dressed, and fun to be around. He nicknamed me "Smiley." He said I had a beautiful smile. He loved my smile, and I was always smiling whenever I was with him. We connected right from the start and had good chemistry together in the beginning. That eventually changed when I found out that he, in fact, already had a girlfriend who he'd been dating for quite some time.

Shortly after finding out about his girlfriend, I learned that I was pregnant again with his first child and my third. A couple of months later, I found out that his long-term girlfriend was pregnant as well. I was having his first daughter, and she was having his first son, literally a couple of months a part. She and I hated each other, had a couple arguments, and were both adamant about keeping our children away from one another. My relationship with Marcus ended by my sixth month of pregnancy because of his other relationship, and we had no further dealings with one another outside of the baby we'd conceived.

I had my daughter on June 17, 1993. I named her Maya, and Marcus' other girlfriend delivered her son, Little Marcus, on August 30, 1993. Eventually she and I ceased our feud, talked and came to an agreement about allowing our kids to grow up having a relationship with one another without letting our personal feelings get in the way. That's exactly what we did. We let our children bond, even grew to love one another's child as well. Marcus was crazy about and loved our daughter. He was a good dad to our baby girl. Although he and I didn't make it together, it never stopped him from providing for and being consistently involved in her life. I have nothing bad to say about him, and I thank him for being there for us when we needed him.

Following old behavior patterns of jumping from relationship to relationship, I soon started dating Kevin before my daughter was a year old. He and I dated approximately three years. During that time, there was a lot of physical, verbal, and emotional abuse. Kevin was quiet mannered and peaceful, as long as he was completely sober. Yet, when he started drinking, it brought out a volatile side of him.

During our three years together, Kevin broke my nose, blacked my eyes on several occasions, threw me down a flight of concrete stairs, stomped me, kicked me in the head, and even shot at me. It had gotten so violent and dangerous between us, and he was beating me so badly that I ended up stabbing him once in the stomach, nearly killing him. That incident resulted in him being operated on and hospitalized for days. On another occasion, during a fight, I stabbed him multiple times all over his upper torso, which resulted in multiple stitches. Both times, he prevented me from going to jail by telling the emergency room doctors and the police that someone else had stabbed him.

After that last incident, I had to get out of the relationship, or somebody was going to end up dead. There were several more fights before we eventually broke up, and I moved again. I was on a search for something or someone to fill the void I had been feeling for many years. That search landed me right in the middle of more toxic and violent relationships.

I began clubbing and running with people who drank and snorted cocaine. I eventually started engaging in those same activities and behaviors. I soon met Big Mike in a nightclub. He was from Chattanooga. The guy was like 6'3, 275 pounds, very handsome, and had that street thug mentality. That was something I was attracted to from the very start. Big Mike was a known weed supplier around town, and he ran with a group of shady and dangerous individuals from Atlanta. It didn't take long for me to discover that Big Mike was shady too.

I was often at Big Mike's house hanging out with him when these individuals would come by and make drug deals. About a month into seeing one another, Big Mike came by my house and asked me if I'd do him a favor. He needed me to drive his car to his house to grab a couple of duffle bags with some clothes he'd packed. He said the police were out riding heavy. He was dirty and didn't want to risk being pulled over. Me, being gullible and naïve, agreed to go. It was no big deal. I didn't have a license, but I was a female, so they wouldn't pay me much attention. Besides I was only going to get his clothes. It wasn't like I was picking up drugs or anything.

> Before I could open the driver's door and step out, I was surrounded by three cars. There was one in front of me, one in the back, and one on the side.

When I pulled up to his house, I noticed it was extremely dark in and around the house. I didn't think anything of it and proceeded to park. Before I could open the driver's door and step out, I was surrounded by three cars. There was one in front of me, one in the back, and one on the side. About six black guys jumped out wearing ski masks with guns yelling, "Where that nigga at?"

I was terrified. My heart was beating out of my chest, and I didn't know what to do, who they were, what exactly to say, or what was going on. One of them seemed to be the leader, and he was the most aggressive and scariest of them all. Again, he asked, "Where is that nigga. Don't say you don't know cause you're driving his car?"

I immediately said, "He's at my house. I'm just here because he asked me to come get him some clothes."

He then said, "Drive and take me to him."

He and one of the other dudes got in the car with me, and the other ones got back in their cars and followed us back to my house. While on our way, the leader told me they wouldn't hurt me and explained why they were looking for him. Big Mike had run off with 50 pounds of weed and a lot of money of his. He wanted it back. The drive to my house was only 10 minutes at best, yet it felt like an hour. I was scared to death. If they caught him, it wasn't going to end well. I didn't want to get hurt or involved, but I was stuck dead in the middle of it all.

We arrived at my house, got out of our cars, and began walking towards my apartment when I noticed that all my lights were turned off. Reality set in that Big Mike had set me up. He had used and knowingly put me in danger to protect himself. I was angry, hurt, and just wanted the whole thing to end. I opened my door, and they all bombarded my apartment, turning on every light, looking in the bedrooms, all the closets, cabinets, and drawers. There was no Big Mike, no weed, and no money to be found. He was gone, and they started asking me all kinds of questions I didn't have the answer to. They knew he'd been there, and he'd sent me to his house because I had his car. They told me to tell him they were looking for him and were not going to stop until they got back what belonged to them. Then, they left.

I couldn't believe what had just happened. That man had played me, and I'd come so close to danger. I wasn't in my apartment by myself five minutes when I heard a knock at the door. I thought they had returned, but when I asked who was at the door, I heard Mike's voice. He had been right outside of my apartment hiding in the bushes the entire time, and those dudes ransacked my apartment. He heard their conversation as they were heading to their cars.

We began arguing. He was mad at me for telling them where he was and felt like I had betrayed and tried to set him up to be killed. I followed him outside to his car where the argument escalated. Big Mike wore a huge ring on his hand, and he hit me in the forehead with that closed fist, splitting it open, straight down the middle. Blood was spewing everywhere, and I began to scream. A friend of mine ran outside where she found me lying on the ground, and Big Mike had his foot drawn back about to kick me in the head. I could hear her screaming while he continued punching me in the face.

She screamed, "No stop, Mike. You're going to kill her!"

I screamed, "Help me, somebody help me!"

My friend called the police after he took off and left in his car. I lay there screaming, "Please call my mama."

The police, paramedics, and my mother all arrived at what seemed like the same time. I remember seeing the sheer terror on my mother's face when she saw me in the back of the ambulance. I ended up needing several stitches in my forehead. I had busted lips, scratches, and two black eyes. I took out a warrant on Big Mike for assaulting me, but they couldn't locate him to arrest him. I never told the police about the events of that night and what we were fighting about because I didn't want it to lead to them investigating those dudes who'd basically kidnapped and forced me to take them to my apartment. I didn't want to get killed for being a snitch. So, I made up another story about why we had been fighting. I cried for days in disbelief of it all and how he had the audacity to blame and jump on me for something that he did wrong. *How could he put me in that position?* I was done with him, and I meant it. I wasn't in love with him. We hadn't been dating long at all.

A couple of days went by before Mike started calling and begging me to forgive and talk to him. I refused and hung up in his face each time he called. Caller I.D. didn't help because he called me from different numbers, and the calls became more frequent at all different times of the day and night. Then, the stalking began. He would call my phone and tell me to look out the window. He would be standing outside. It had gotten so bad and frightening that I went to get a restraining order. I also went to my mom's for a while because I was afraid of staying at home anymore.

The police eventually caught him in Chattanooga, Tennessee where he was from originally, and he was ordered to stay away from me. I don't know whatever came of that situation with the drug dealer he took the weed from, but I never heard from Big Mike again after that. Just as I'd always done after a failed relationship, I moved again

Love Found Me

CHAPTER 8

This was a new beginning for me. I was living in a new apartment complex, and I had a plan. My oldest son, Jarret, had come back home to live with me and I had sole custody of my baby girl, Maya. I wanted to start being a better mom, get a steady job, and stay out of toxic relationships. I went out occasionally but not like in the past, and I was no longer snorting cocaine and bringing different men home. I had more responsibilities with two of my three children in the home. I could no longer live the way I had before.

It was just my kids and I for the first few years. I wasn't involved with anyone seriously and wasn't thinking about it. A childhood friend and I, who lived in the same apartment complex, would often sit outside while the kids played. One day, she said she knew this guy who had been asking about me. He wanted to meet and get to know me. I asked who he was, what he was about, and where he knew me from to say he wanted to get to know me?. She said he'd been seeing me around and just wanted to meet me, so I agreed, and she set it up.

The next day she called my house and told me he was there at her house and wanted me to come over, so I did. His name was J.D. He was very handsome, neatly dressed in a button-down Tommy Hilfiger shirt, pants, and shoes. He was somewhat shy or maybe just nervous to meet me for the first time, yet he was extremely charming. I immediately noticed J.D. was cut from a different cloth. He was different from the others I'd met and dated before him. He didn't have visible tattoos, sagging pants, braids, gold chains, or gold teeth. He was clean cut, had a low fade, was well dressed, very well mannered, and more impressive. In addition, he didn't have any kids.

> I could no longer live the way I had before.

J.D. was 4 years younger than me, but you couldn't tell it, and I often forgot because of his level of maturity. Knoxville is small and I had never heard of or seen him before. His name was not popular in street gossip. We clicked instantly, and I later gave him my number and eventually invited him to my apartment so we could better talk in private and get to know one another.

We started going out on dates, going for rides, and spending more time with each other. One evening, he came to see me. That was one of the most beautiful and memorable experiences I had with him. That night we talked for hours. He let me know that he sold and smoked weed. I was okay with that. I had dated men who were into far heavier illegal activities. The most beautiful and memorable moments took place in my bedroom. We were fully dressed, watched movies, and stayed up talking and laughing late into the midnight hour. I then got up to go change into something a little sexier and more relaxing. When I climbed back into bed, he was still fully dressed. He put his arms around me, held me close, and we both fell asleep with him holding me in his arms all night without him making any sexual advances.

That was the night I knew real love had found me, and I had found it! After that, we were inseparable, best friends, in love, and very happy. We had so much in common. We liked the same foods, the same T.V. shows, movies, and music. Jagged Edge was our favorite group, and every time we'd get in the car together, he'd play "I GOTTA BE." Even today when I hear it, I instantly think of him and have to hold back the tears in my eyes.

We were so compatible and connected that when we'd decide to go to a club or concert somewhere, we'd go to the mall to get something new to wear. To save some time, we'd split up and go our separate ways to shop and have a designated time and place in the mall where we would meet. We'd get all the way home, pull our clothes out of the bags, and discover, without ever planning or even discussing what colors we wanted to wear, we'd have the same identical colors each time. We'd be color coordinated from head to toe, and no one would've ever guessed or thought we did not plan it.

There would be times that I'd touch him on his forearm,

and he'd say, "Every time you touch me, you give me chills." He'd pull back, hold his arms out, and there would literally be 100's of tiny chill bumps everywhere, and we'd just hug and giggle like teenagers. Just like any relationship, we soon had our first disagreement. Keep in mind, I was accustomed to dysfunction, toxicity, and violence. I had never been in a relationship where the man didn't hit or verbally abuse me. Because of that, I began to hit him, expecting for him to hit me back. He grabbed me, held me tight, and said, "No, Tameka. I'm not going to hit you. Stop it!" I wouldn't stop hitting him so he broke free from me and left. He later returned to get his things. He wasn't used to that type of foolishness, and he wanted no parts in it.

I knew I had messed up. I also knew J.D. was different. I loved him, and I couldn't lose him. I cried and begged him not to go. After talking and things calming down, he decided he didn't want to let go of me either and agreed to give it another chance. Needless to say, if I wanted to keep him, I had to get myself under control and figure out a better way to resolve issues. We eventually grew closer, he moved in, and we became inseparable. We eventually moved out of the apartment complex and into our first house. He and the kids became close, and he took on the role of being their father. We were involved with their school activities, homework, birthdays, Christmas, and more. Anything involving the kids, he was there for it.

We were living a good life. I had help with the kids emotionally, physically, and financially. Neither of us were working at the time, so I kind of figured he was dealing in more than just weed. He later told me he not only sold weed. He also sold dope. He just never did anything illegal in front of the kids or ever allowed anyone to come to our home under those circumstances.

A few more years went by. Then, we both got some shocking and unexpected news. I had missed my period, yet I didn't think anything of it because I had gotten my tubes tide after my third child. I just figured I was late. I began having some abdominal pains a few days later, and J.D. took me to the emergency room. Once there, they ran a series of tests. When the doctor walked in and began to go over the results, we were both shocked, happy, and concerned. I was pregnant, but my tubes had been tied for years. *How can this be?* I thought.

> I had to undergo an emergency surgery.

J.D. stood up, put his arms around me, and we listened to the doctor. He had me go for a follow up to see an OB/GYN the next day. They ran further tests and confirmed it was in fact an ectopic pregnancy. The OB/GYN ordered a human chorionic gonadotropin (HCB) test to further confirm if I was pregnant. The level of this hormone increases during pregnancy, so they tested me that day. I returned a few days later for them to compare the levels, to see if they were increasing or not.

When I returned, the levels had not increased, and I had to undergo an emergency surgery to remove my right fallopian tube before it ruptured and possibly killed me. That turn of events changed our relationship, my life, and opened Pandora's Box.

Love Found Me Part 2

CHAPTER 9

On Thanksgiving Eve, J.D. had to take a trip out of town to handle some business. I stayed home with the kids, so I could prepare Thanksgiving dinner for my little family. While cooking, I decided to load up the kids and make a run to the grocery store to get some last-minute things I needed for our family feast. I remembered leaving the living room and kitchen lights on because I had been right in the middle of cooking.

The kids and I left and were gone maybe an hour at most. When we returned, I didn't notice anything out of the ordinary, so we proceeded to get the groceries out of the car and head inside. Our backdoor was on the right side of the house, and we didn't have a driveway, so we had to park directly in the front. On the front door, J.D. had a security door installed for added protection and was going to have one installed on the backdoor, but we didn't make it to that point.

I unlocked the storm door and went inside first, the kids following behind me. Once I stepped into my living room, I remembered thinking how dark it was and how I knew I had left the lights on. As we proceeded to the kitchen and before I could reach to turn the light on, I could feel the extremely strong presence that someone besides us was in the house. I felt we were in danger, and we needed to run out of the house. I reached out to feel for my kids, pushed them back towards the living room, and yelled, "Get out of the house now."

We all made it out safely, and I immediately called J.D. to tell him what was going on. He told me to call 911 and he was calling his brother to have him come over to stay with us. The reason I didn't call the police first was because I didn't know if there was anything illegal in there, and I didn't want to draw attention to J.D. or our home.

The police soon arrived, along with his brother. They went in to search the house when they discovered the backdoor had been kicked open. After making sure the house was clear, they had me come inside to see if anything of value had been taken. The house was a wreck. They had ransacked every room except my daughter's. I let the police know nothing of real value had been taken.

Of course, that aroused their suspicion. I mean no one would break in just to break in and make a mess. They asked if I had any clue what they could've been looking for and I said no. They took pictures and did the fingerprint procedure just in case something came of the situation.

When they left, I called J.D. back to let him know the handgun we kept for protection had been taken. After he calmed me down, he let me know he would be home first thing the next morning. His brother had someone to come secure the backdoor while I began cleaning up. When I went into the laundry room, which was in my son's bedroom and where the backdoor was located, I discovered a clothes basket with dirty white clothes in it. I also saw an adult size print from the bottom of men's tennis shoes on top of the clothes. It dawned on me what had actually happened.

Upon arriving home, there must've been a lookout, someone watching out the front to see when I or J.D. would be pulling up. They couldn't run out of the side without risking me or the kids seeing them, so they hid. That's why I felt the eerie strong presence of someone inside of the house when I walked to the kitchen, which was literally 3 to 4 steps away from my son's bedroom where they were hiding.

All I could do was thank God for His discernment and for protecting us. The next morning JD came home. We talked about what happened. He promised to get us out of there and not take any more trips until we moved.

Despite the break-in, we had a wonderful Thanksgiving. It was the first time I had cooked my own family dinner for Thanksgiving, and we ate at home, rather than going to my or his mom's.

About a month later J.D. was promoting a show in Chattanooga, Tennessee. The artist was a new up and coming rap icon, T.I. J.D. had rented a limousine service and allowed me to invite one of my childhood friends and her boyfriend to accompany us. Her boyfriend was known for robbery and break-ins but that didn't matter to us because he was from the same neighborhood where we'd grown up. We knew him very well besides the fact that he was my friend's boyfriend at the time.

J.D. was a free hearted person who didn't mind doing things like showing people a great time. Whenever he did it, he did it big. He had already booked a presidential suite that had two rooms in it, and that's where we stayed after the show and a night of partying. They didn't have to pay for anything. During our ride home in the limousine the next day, we talked to them about the break-in the month prior, and we still didn't know who was behind it.

Once we arrived back in Knoxville, we were dropping my friend's boyfriend off first when he said he had something he wanted and needed to tell us. He confessed that he was in fact one of the people who had kicked our door open in an attempt to rob our house. We were shocked and completely caught off guard by his confession. What he said next not only shocked us but broke my heart. He said one of my close relatives set the whole thing up. He swore he had no idea it was our house. All he knew was it was a lick and was told there was a lot of dope, weed, and money in our house. He swore on his life it wasn't until he got inside and saw all our pictures that he realized it was ours. He told us he was sorry, and he felt bad about it. He wanted to tell us last night, but it wasn't the right time.

His confession made me believe he was remorseful, felt horrible about it, and was being honest about who came to him with the robbery plan. J.D. wasn't the violent type, but he was no punk either. He just wasn't on that. No one he loved was hurt, and nothing but a handgun was taken, so we thanked him for telling us the truth and owning his part in it. After all, he didn't have to, and we probably wouldn't have ever known the truth had he not told us.

I eventually confronted the close relative about what my friend's boyfriend confessed to us. Of course, he got upset and denied it. I knew him too well, and I knew he was lying about his involvement. We didn't speak for a couple of years behind that, but I'd known him my whole life. He was my blood, my family. I loved him and couldn't believe he'd do that to me. Eventually, I forgave him for it, and J.D. and I just let the whole thing go because he'd never admit to being involved, and he didn't have to because deep down I knew he was.

I thought the situation would cause some turbulence in my relationship with J. D. but it didn't. In fact, it seemed to have brought us closer together. I had a job working for a collection agency during that time when I got a call from J.D. telling me to meet him at the Kroger, a grocery store not too far from where I worked. I met him there. He was already standing outside of his car waiting for me. He walked over towards me telling me to get out of the car. As we approached each other, J.D. reached into his pocket and pulled out a small gift box. Inside of it was the most beautiful ring I'd ever seen. It was a 2.3 carat diamond. Back in the early 2000's, a 2.3 carat diamond ring was considered huge. Well, at least to me it was because I'd never owned a real diamond ring of any size in my life. He took it out of the box and said, "Just because I love you. You keep acting right and your engagement ring will be bigger than this."

Oh, I was on top of the world. I don't even think I got lunch that day because I was full of love and joy. Later that same evening, when I got off work, J.D. called me again to ask where I was. I told him I was just getting off. He told me to meet him at home. When I pulled up, I saw a beautiful 2002, silver four-door Cadillac DeVille.

He said, "Dang that's pretty. Whoever is driving that sure is riding pretty." He continued, "You like that?"

I said, "Yes!"

Then he replied, "Here you go. It's yours," and handed me

the keys.

I said, "Stop lying." Then, I jumped out and ran to the car. I couldn't believe he'd given me my very first diamond ring earlier and a caddy. Man, you're talking about on top of the world. I was on the tip top of it! Nothing else could top what he'd just done all in one day, except for asking me to marry him.

The very next day he told me we were going to meet with a lady about a house. He'd promised me to move us out of the house that had been broken into, and he was ready to do just that. The following day came, and we pulled up to this newly built subdivision in West Knoxville. It was and still to this day is away from the inner city, a low crime area, and where people who work in the corporate world live. They at least have a 6-figure income or make a lot of money illegally. Back then, in the streets, it was considered Big Boy status if you could afford to live down west without a housing voucher or any type of governmental assistance.

We pulled into one of the cul-de-sacs and into a driveway with a garage. When the garage door opened, I looked at him with my eyes big as fifty cent pieces. I began screaming with more joy. We weren't meeting anyone there to look at the house. He had already met with the owner and gotten us approved to move in. These were $250,000 or more homes, and we were about to move into one. It was equivalent to moving into a mansion in our minds because we'd both grew up in housing projects.

The house had a garage, which led into the kitchen. It had 2 full bathrooms upstairs, a 1/2-bathroom downstairs, the kitchen had an island, a laundry room, a living room with a fireplace, and the back door was in the dining room, which led to a huge wooden patio and a huge backyard. It also had an office, den, and a winding staircase that led to the 3 bedrooms upstairs. Each room had walk in closets. The kids' bedrooms both had doors leading to the bathroom they'd share, and our bedroom was the size of an efficiency apartment. It had a cathedral ceiling, a huge walk-in closet, and our bathroom was my favorite part of the house. It had a separate shower, a jacuzzi bathtub, his and her sinks on opposite sides, and two huge windows, one being right beside of the bathtub.

> it reminded me of all the times we used to go riding through beautiful neighborhoods down west just to look at the beautiful homes.

It was absolutely a dream home for us for sure, and it reminded me of all the times we used to go riding through beautiful neighborhoods down west just to look at the beautiful homes and talk about one day owning one. J.D. was making the dream come true in a sense. No, we weren't buying it, but we were going to be living in it as if we owned it. We were expected to move-in by the weekend, and he had more surprises in store for me. He took me furniture shopping. Every stick of furniture in our house upon moving in was brand new, and it was absolutely gorgeous, the best of the best. I remember seeing this gorgeous dining room furniture that had padded high backed chairs, but JD told me it was a little too expensive. I understood. After all, I looked at all he had bought and done for me in just a few days, so I didn't think about complaining.

The weekend came, and it was time to move into our beautiful new place. Once we pulled up, J.D. told us to enter the house through the back patio door, so we wouldn't scratch up the wooden floors in the foyer. The rest of the house had brand new carpeting, and he didn't want to risk tracking it with dirt. I opened that back door and screamed. That gorgeous dining room set I wanted so badly was sitting there waiting for me. J.D. had gone back to the furniture store, paid cash for it, and had it delivered a day before we got there.

I couldn't believe I had this amazing man who loved me and my kids whom he did not father, but he did love them. We were living in such a beautiful neighborhood, in such a beautiful house. He wanted us to have the absolute best of everything and we did. J.D. and I had a beautiful relationship. We were best friends, as well as lovers, and he was so romantic. He was the first man to ever show me what romance was and what it felt like by often surprising me with romantic evenings out or at home.

One of the things we used to like to do was go buy all the new movie releases that would come out every week at Walmart. I can remember us watching the movie Love & Basketball together when it came out. One of the songs on the soundtrack was "A Woman's Work" by Maxwell. We both absolutely fell in love with that song. During our happier times, we would play it often while riding in the car together and holding hands. There was nothing but sheer love and joy for a long time.

Unfortunately, one the old demons of my past reappeared, and I found myself taking and abusing pain pills again. My relapse began to cause a lot of strain and emotional distance in our relationship. I was pulling away from him and back into the deep abyss of opiate addiction I'd fought so hard to come out of. One time, after a huge fight, J.D. came home, went to our CD player, and started playing "A Woman's Work." He got down on his knees in front of me and began to cry. What he said next let me know he was feeling despair, helpless, and he was losing me to my addiction. "Please come back to me," he said. We held one another, and we both cried our hearts out.

Everything in me wanted to because I loved him. I loved us, and everything in me wanted to go back to being the woman I was before I ever became addicted to prescription pain medicine, but I had lost my way, and I didn't know how to. Eventually my opiate abuse caused us to argue more than ever. At times, he'd get so mad, leave the house, and stay gone for days. During this time, his business was starting to thrive. We didn't spend as much time together as we'd always done because he was busy promoting the shows he was bringing to Knoxville and other cities.

Up to this point, J.D. and I were inseparable. Whenever you saw him, you saw me and vice versa, but it stopped being that way. With the changes he was noticing in me, I, too, started gradually noticing more changes in him, his patterns, and behavior. We stopped having as much sex as in the past. He started giving me more money to go do things for fun with the kids without him. It began to feel as if he was distracting me or keeping me occupied so to speak. Although in my spirit, I felt he was seeing someone else, I never questioned it. I never questioned it because the five years we'd been together I hadn't so much as heard a rumor he had been unfaithful. Absolutely nothing had ever been said to me about him being involved with other women.

The emotional and physical distance between us started creating a void. I felt I was missing something. I began feeling neglected, unwanted, and I thought that neither of us were happy being together anymore. That was my selfish and immature way of thinking at the time. Looking back (hindsight 20/20), now that I'm older and drug free, I can see I had been emotionally and physically unavailable to or for him first. I wish I'd seen it back then, but I didn't have the emotional, mental, or MORE IMPORTANLY the spiritual capacity to see it during that time.

The kids were gone one weekend. J.D. had some important business to take care of, so I decided to go visit a cousin in Nashville. During my visit (the first trip I'd taken by myself in a very long time without J.D.), I felt sort of free. I wanted to let loose and enjoy every moment of it. My cousin and I decided to go out to a nightclub to listen to music and have drinks when I met Antwan. He sparked an old interest that I once had in men before I met J.D. I used to be attracted to street dudes, the rough type. In my mind and heart, I didn't want it to go any further than simple conversation. We had a couple of drinks, exchanged numbers, and that was the end of it.

Sunday morning before returning to Knoxville, Antwan called me. I realized that I had given him my number and was about to return home. He couldn't be calling me while I was at home, so I had to let him know about J.D. He was very understanding of it, promised not to call me, and would wait for my calls only. We talked a little bit longer, said our goodbyes, and I left Nashville. I returned home to my family and thought nothing more of my trip or the fact that I had met someone and given my number to him.

Upon returning home, I noticed J.D. becoming even more distant than before. I started noticing him taking his phone into the bathroom with him, something that was out of the ordinary. The feeling that something wasn't right only grew more intense, and that's when things really started to go terribly wrong. J.D. was spending an awful lot of time on a local college campus. I knew he had some friends he did business with who went to the college, but it was something else. I just couldn't put my finger on it.

One day, he told me he needed to go to the Walgreens located on the campus to have some flyers printed off for one of his shows he was having. I thought nothing of it originally, but then it dawned on me, "There are several other Walgreens locations closer to us. Why did he need to go to that one?" I decided to get in my car and drive to that location. Once I got there, I noticed his car wasn't there, so I called him. I asked him where he was, and he lied to me. He said he was there, but he absolutely wasn't because I was there sitting in the parking lot. The parking lot was small, and there was only one way in and out of it. There was no way I could have missed him.

I never let him know I was there at that location. Before we hung up the phone, he told me he needed to make a couple of more stops before he'd be home. I left feeling sad, angry, and in disbelief that was happening. It confirmed my suspicion. Why else would he lie? I knew him too well, and I could tell he was lying to me.

J.D. had a show come up and a local venue here in Knoxville, and we had gone to the show together as usual, but this time was different. He kept disappearing in the club and returning, but his behavior was odd. I remember seeing these females who were sisters there. They came to sit at a table in THE

VIP section not too far from us. Every time I would look up, they'd be staring at me. One of them got up from the table and walked through the crowd. A few minutes later J.D. walked off again. I didn't think anything of it at the time because he was the one hosting the show, so I wrote it off to him handling business.

I later found out, after our breakup, he had been in fact seeing one of those sisters at the show that night while we were still together. He had given them VIP tickets to be seated near us. A few weeks after that show, J.D. and I had become increasingly more emotionally and sexually distant from one another. He was there physically, but emotionally he had become almost unavailable. I was feeling lonely and neglected when I got an unsuspecting phone call from Antwan.

I had forgotten I'd given him the number, so I was surprised and flattered to hear from him. That phone call led to more. Eventually, I found myself sneaking away just to talk to him for a few minutes. I made plans to return to Nashville to see him, using my cousin as an excuse for my second visit. When I arrived, I stayed with Antwan for the weekend. Before leaving, I told him it might cause suspicion if I kept coming back and forth. That's when he decided to come to Knoxville a few weeks later. I didn't know how I was going to pull that off. I had never stayed out all night without J.D. and didn't know how I would be able to explain it if I did. I tried calling Antwan and canceling that idea, but he was determined to come and wasn't taking no for an answer. *Well, I guess I'll do to J.D. what he's done to me in the past*, I thought. I'll start an argument, get really upset, and use that as my excuse to stay out all night.

> Well, I guess I'll do to J.D. what he's done to me in the past,

The weekend came, and Antwan called me earlier in the day to let me know he was on his way. Nashville is only a three-hour drive, so I had to get things ready fast before he arrived. J.D. and I ended up having an argument about something without me having to start one intentionally. He left the house. I thought he was going to stay gone like he'd started doing after a big argument, only this time he didn't.

While he was gone, I went to our bathroom to take a bath and get ready. While in the tub, I went through the yellow pages to make reservations for a hotel for the weekend. After taking a bath, getting dressed, dropping the kids off, and meeting Antwan at a designated location, we went to the hotel and stayed all night. While there, I felt so guilty and realized he wasn't who I wanted to be with, so I told him. I was about to leave to go back home when a girlfriend of mine called to tell me that J.D. was calling around and out riding around looking for me. She asked where I was. Because I thought I could trust her, I told her about Antwan. I had no clue one of J.D.'s friends was right there with her at the time we were having that discussion. He called J.D. and told him he overheard our conversation but didn't know exactly which hotel I was at.

J.D. began calling my phone back-to-back. I answered and could hear him yelling and asking where I was and with whom was I with? I hung up in his face and knew I couldn't go home at that point! I could tell he knew something, and I had to get my explanation together, so I ended up staying the night at the hotel after telling Antwan he had to leave because J.D. was out looking for me. I didn't know what would happen if he found me.

Antwan eventually left, and I could tell that he was scared too. He wasn't from our area, didn't know anyone but me, and he didn't know what was going to happen. When the sun came up, I left the hotel, praying all the way home for J.D. not to be there when I arrived.

I pulled into the garage and ran inside when the house phone began to ring. It was my mom telling me that J.D. knew I had been at the hotel. She named the hotel and told me he'd seen my car. My heart sank. I walked into the bathroom and noticed I had left the phone book wide open on *HOTELS*. Then, I began trembling with fear, regret, and dread. All of sudden, I heard the garage door opening. I could hear J.D. trampling through the house and up the stairs towards our bedroom. I stood there with my eyes big and mouth wide open, but nothing was coming out.

He headed straight for me, grabbed the house phone from me, took the cord and wrapped it around my neck. Then, he began to pull yelling, "What have you done Tameka, why?" I guess he realized what he was doing and immediately released me and left the house! Keep in mind, he was a man who'd never been violent with me in the past. He had never so much as called me out of my name one time, and that was the headspace that he was in.

When he finally left the house, I broke down crying. I tried to call him, and he'd only answer to say, "I hate you" and hang up. I didn't know what to do, but I made matters even worse by calling the police on him. I told them he'd strangled me with the phone cord and took an order of protection out on him. After doing it, I instantly regretted it. I knew he'd never physically harm me. His reaction was triggered from having his heart broken, being disrespected, humiliated, and betrayed. We were both immature, made terrible judgement calls, and did things to each other we could never take back.

Me cheating was one thing, but I called the police on the man who truly loved me and my kids and who took damn good care of us. There was no turning back. He couldn't forgive me for it. I never went to court. As far as I know, they threw the matter out due to lack of evidence and no witnesses. That was the end of the love that had found me. J.D. and I broke up, and Pandora's box began to open.

Before I move along with my story, I have a message for the women. Sometimes as women, we can get caught up in how a man makes us feel, what he is or isn't doing, what we want, how we want it, and when we want it. However, we never stop to think about their needs and if we're doing what we can to meet them. We always want the man to be who he was when we first fell in love with him, but we stop being who we were when he fell in love with us. We want to fix him instead of working on what is wrong within ourselves.

The mistake we make is expecting a man to make us happy. Our happiness is no one's responsibility but our own. They can only add to or take away from it, but we've got to find our own happiness within. Joy comes from the Lord, and nobody can give it to us, nor can they take it away! "Seek ye first the Kingdom of God and His righteousness, and all of these things shall be added unto you" (Matthew 6:33).

Another mistake some women make is being totally dependent on a man financially, which gives him entirely too much power over them. There's nothing wrong with having a dependable man, but there is something wrong with you being codependent. Your independence as a responsible woman should always go hand in hand with his dependability. If he decides to leave you today, what and when you eat should never be contingent upon his presence.

Pandora's Box

CHAPTER 10

Pandora's Box Part 1

Over the next few weeks and months, things between us got increasingly worse. After the situation with me getting caught cheating and involving the police, J.D. became someone that I did not recognize at all. Because I had no job and was completely codependent upon him, I had no way to pay the $1200 a month rent. Therefore, there was no other choice than to apply for Section 8 emergency housing. I had those kids, and I was responsible for providing for them by making sure they had a place to live, as well as pay a car note, other bills, and supply my raging pain pill addiction. J.D. eventually ended up letting go of the car notes, which resulted in the Cadillac being repossessed from me in broad daylight while I was at a gas station. They had tracked me down, followed me, and waited for me to go into the store to take possession of the vehicle. That was another humiliating, scary, and very hurtful experience for me.

Soon after that, I moved out of the beautiful house in the predominantly white, middle-class neighborhood. I was back on government assistance, without a car, no money, and nothing but me and my kids. The only thing we had left was each other. Thank God I still had brand spanking new furniture I could use to furnish our new place. J.D. even had his attorney reach out to me to inform me of what furniture he wanted back. I absolutely refused to give him anything. My way of thinking at the time was that it was easier for him to start over. He was by himself, he was a man, and he had all the money.

We had very short break ups in the past, which never lasted for more than a week, and we'd always end up working it out and getting back together. That was our worst fight and breakup ever, yet I thought we'd somehow work it out and get back together. Nothing or no one could've ever prepared me for the heartache, pain, and devastation of our relationship ending for good. It felt like someone I loved suddenly and unexpectedly passed away.

J.D. wouldn't talk to me and got his number changed, only calling me from a private number whenever he wanted to talk to me or ask if the kids needed anything. I'd ride around looking for him, call his mom, his brother, and some of our mutual friends. I begged them to get him to at least talk to me, so I could try to explain myself. I guess there was no good explanation for my cheating, lying, betraying, embarrassing, and then calling the police on him. He had such a close relationship and bond with the kids that he'd only come by the house to check on them to make sure they were okay, but that was it. He wanted nothing else to do with me at all.

My great grandmother passed away. She was very fond of J.D., and he was very fond of her. Out of him wanting to pay his respects for my great grandmother's passing, he agreed to accompany me and the kids to the funeral. After the funeral, everyone went to one of my relatives for the repast. During the funeral procession and our drive to the repast, I don't think he said more than five words to me, which made my great grandmother's passing even worse. Not only was I grieving her death, but I was also literally, physically, mentally spiritually, and emotionally grieving the death of my five-year relationship to the man I loved more than anything.

I regretted the stupid decision I made to jeopardize our love and relationship for something or someone temporary. I thought I wasn't happy anymore. I thought I was tired of J.D. I thought I was missing something. I thought the grass was greener on the other side, but I was wrong about everything.

On his way to take me and the kids home, he asked the kids if they wanted anything from the store. He stopped at a gas station and went inside. When he got out of the truck, I heard a cellphone ring. When I looked around the truck to see if I could find it, I noticed one was in the driver's side door. *So, he has two cellphones now,* I thought. *Why was he hiding it?* Without much thought, I reached over, grabbed it, turned the ringer off, and stuck it in my purse.

He returned to the truck and took us home. Once we pulled up in the driveway, I told the kids to go inside so J.D. and I could talk in private. He then said, "I don't want to talk. I have somewhere to be." He was rushing me out of his truck. Once he left, I went inside and turned the cellphone back on and discovered several text messages from other women. One of them he had been texting frequently. From the content of the text, he was involved with her. I called the number, introduced myself to the chic, and we began talking. She went on to tell me that she knew me, and she and J.D. had been involved for quite some time, even during our relationship, long before I ever thought about cheating and getting caught. She then had the nerve to tell me how much J.D. loved me, how he made it clear to her from the beginning that he wasn't leaving me for her, and nothing could ever get back to me about the two of them messing around.

> I called the number, introduced myself to the chic, and we began talking.

She explained how they met and when they had the time to hook up. Remember, he and I were always together for the most part until I got really hooked on those pills and would sleep most of the day away. During and after our conversation, I started putting everything together and realized he'd been cheating right under my nose. Those times I had my suspicions, I was right. That explained the distance between us sexually and emotionally. It explained how the times started becoming more frequent that we'd get into it. He'd get mad enough at me to stay gone 2-3 nights at a time, never answering his phone for me. Then, he'd come back home to make up with me as if we both just needed some space apart.

Remember the business trip he'd taken Thanksgiving Eve, the night our house was broken into? Well, she knew about that too because she had been with him the whole time, when I called frantically to tell him what had happened. After that phone call with her, I found out from other people about all the others he'd been seeing. With the discovery of each one came even more heartache and loss of control over my drug use. I didn't know how to cope. I had never experienced a break-up like that before, and I had to find a way to try and numb the pain.

I started going around a cousin of mine just to hang out and be around other people, which was an attempt to escape the reality of my world. My cousin was older and was the life of any party she attended. She and I had partied together in the past and snorted cocaine, but she also smoked crack crushed up and rolled together in a cigar with cigarette tobacco. This same cousin, for many years prior to this, had been strung out on the crack pipe. In everybody's mind, I think they believed smoking it this way wasn't as bad.

One day, I stopped by her house while she and her husband were in the middle of drinking and smoking one of those cigarettes. I just wanted to talk, vent, and cry about everything that was going on with J.D. and me. I ended up asking to try one of her loaded cigarettes. That was my very first time ever trying crack. It not only made me feel better emotionally for the moment, but it also took my mind off everything. That was the day the door to Pandora's Box opened and invited me in.

A couple months had gone by and the pain from my break-up with J.D. became increasingly worse. My depression was causing me to lose weight from not being able to eat. I couldn't sleep, and all I could do was cry. I cried every single day for 365 days straight. I lay on the floor balled up in a fetal position and begged God to give him back to me. That was one of the first times I ever truly felt like giving up, and I eventually did.

I stopped taking the pain pills completely because I couldn't afford to buy them. For me, it was more affordable to buy a crack rock, cigars, use tobacco from my cigarettes, and get high that way. Smoking loaded cigars was my new high. It felt 100 times better than taking the pills and was easier to come by. When smoking crack, you start making new friends, those who live the same lifestyle as you. These are friends you can get high with without judgement.

That's when I met Lisa. She smoked crack, but she smoked it in a pipe, which used less dope and didn't smell as bad as it did when I smoked it in a cigar. Lisa smoked hers in a crack pipe, and we'd come to each other's house every single day to get high together. My kids would either be asleep or spending the night away from home, which allowed me to get away with it easier.

One night while at my house, she was sitting on the floor smoking her pipe, and I was sitting on my bed smoking crack in my cigars. I looked at her and said those four demonic words, "Let me try that." I wanted to see how it felt to smoke the crack in a pipe. Surely, it couldn't be any better and certainly no more addictive than how I was already smoking it. I couldn't have been more wrong. It was 10xs more effective, powerful, and addictive. The first time I tried it, it grabbed me. It gave me this head rush, an indescribable euphoria that I'd never felt before. I later learned, from experience, that you never get that same exact high you get the very first time when smoking the crack pipe. That is what one ultimately ends up chasing, that VERY FIRST high and not the actual crack rock itself.

Pandora's Box Part 2

The moment I made the decision to try smoking the crack pipe was the moment my life and the lives of those I was responsible for began to spiral completely out of control. I was hanging out more at Lisa's house. She didn't have any small kids, and her house was the go-to spot for other smokers and dealers. It was a place where I could hangout all day and get high off others, but that changed quickly.

I learned fast that getting high for free was not an option, and the addiction soon required me to fund it myself. I did, at any cost necessary. My oldest son was a teenager and was old enough to be left home alone. I would send my daughter to a

friend of mine's house to hangout while I was off finding a way to get high. Shoplifting became my hustle to cover the expenses of me getting high. Eventually, that wasn't enough. My addiction required more, and it took way more money to cover it. That's when I started selling things out of my house. I sold shoes, clothes, DVD movies, TV's, lamps, and table decor. I began trading the food stamps I was getting for the kids to buy crack.

At the beginning of my crack addiction, I would buy some groceries and trade what was left for crack. Then, I eventually traded all of it for crack. I'd either borrow food or make up excuses to my friends, and my friends would allow my kids to come to their houses to eat with their kids. Looking back, I thought I was fooling everybody, but they knew something terribly wrong was happening. I was only fooling myself and giving up everything I had and loved. I went as far as selling my daughter's stereo system out of her bedroom while she was in school one day. I could tell she was sad by the look on her face. I remember the overwhelming guilt that I felt seeing her look so sad. I promised to make it up to her and get it back. I told her I needed to pay a bill and had to sell it.

The guilt from what I had done and the lie I told her was short lived because of my craving for more crack. I sold everything I could out of our house, except one T.V. in the living room and our main furniture. The only thing left to sell was my son's 87 Chevy Impala that J.D. purchased for him on Christmas a few years prior. I justified it by telling myself he wasn't old enough to drive it legally yet. He didn't have a driver's license. In my mind, I believed I would get it back for him or purchase something even better.

I did the unthinkable. I sold his car. I will never forget the sadness on my son's face. Again, the guilt was overwhelming. I know he cried, but it was too late. I couldn't undo it. I had sold the car and gotten high. Even today, it's still very painful to even write about how I stole from my children, lied to them, neglected them, embarrassed them, and failed them horribly. I had only been smoking the crack pipe for a month, and I had already stooped that low.

Eventually, my oldest brother found out about what I was doing, and he went to my family. He and my aunt Connie came to my house one morning while the kids were still in school. She confronted me and told me she was taking the kids. I loved my kids, and I didn't want to give them up, but I knew it was the best thing for them at that time. Of course, that was the best decision for my addiction. I told my kids they were going to live with Aunt Connie, and they were upset. They loved their Aunt Connie, but she lived in a different town, and neither of us wanted them to go to another city.

I eventually let Maya go live with her dad and his girlfriend, and Jarret went back to stay with my mom. So, the kids were no longer with me. It had finally come to the light that I was getting high. Therefore, I was able to get high at home as much as I could afford to. I remember telling myself, "As long as my mom and kids know, I don't care what anybody else thinks of me."

Along with my addiction progressively getting worse, so were the things I began to experience, see, and do. One evening, I was downstairs in my bedroom alone getting high, and I heard some confusion coming from outside. I tried ignoring it, but the commotion got so loud and was so close that I stopped and looked outside to see what was going on. I went upstairs, opened my front door, and saw 3 or 4 women and 1 guy arguing. I recognized 1 of the younger ladies as my neighbor. I knew the other women were not residents there because I'd been living there for two years, and I knew all of my neighbors.

After listening and watching, it didn't take long for me to figure out that they were having a confrontation over a man. One of the guys was my neighbor's brother, and he was trying to break it up and diffuse the situation. Then, two of the other ladies began to jump my younger neighbor. With all of his might, the brother of my neighbor punched one of the women in her face. I remember yelling, "Don't hit her like that, y'all stop" He hit her to the point of knocking her out. The woman's face swelled, and she staggered backwards. The woman who had accompanied her got on her cell phone to call someone, and they both left in a hurry.

I heard some confusion coming from outside.

Things momentarily got quiet, and I went back inside to finish getting high. About 45 minutes had gone by when something told me to go back upstairs and look out my front door. When I got there, I looked out and saw 3 young black men (2 of whom I recognized and knew from around town) and another I did not recognize. I could tell something was wrong. They were looking for a particular apartment, and one of them appeared to be extremely upset. That's when I noticed a gun in one of their hands.

One of the guys was the son of the woman who had gotten punched by my neighbor's brother, and he was coming to deal with him about it. I knew him fairly well, so I called out to him by his name, but he was extremely angry and wasn't trying to hear anything, so he ignored me. He then beat on one of the apartment doors. When the woman answered, I heard her frantically say, "You have the wrong door. That happened next door."

There were parking spaces filled with several cars for tenants located directly beside the building, and it sat on a hill. After the three young men realized the door they were looking for was right next to the one where they stood, they proceeded to run to it. By this time, the girl's brother got out of his car with a gun in his hand and quietly ran down the hill, coming up behind them. It was like a movie scene. Everything was happening quickly, and I didn't know whether to scream or to just be quiet. But I mustered enough courage to call out his name.

When I called his name, I yelled, "Wait, stop, let me talk to you." I wanted to try to calm him down and diffuse the situation somehow. I had his attention for maybe three seconds, but the rage overtook his mind and attention. Next, he kicked on the door two good times. The door swung open, and he went in first. One of the guys with him ran in behind him. Before the third one had time to reach the door, the girl's brother grabbed him from behind, held the gun to his head, and walked his body closer to the door, using him as a human shield. He spoke a few words, then fired shots into the apartment, turned the guy loose, pushed him inside, and took off running. I heard screams. A few seconds went by, and two of the guys ran from the apartment. They jumped over a railing and ran away. The son of the woman who had gotten punched in the face did not come out with them.

I frantically ran to my neighbor's porch to see if she'd been shot. When I saw him lying on the floor by the front door, I was shocked. The girl stood there with her toddler son in her arms screaming hysterically. She ran out screaming for someone to call 911, and I stepped inside to see if and where the man had been shot. He was on his back, and his eyes were wide open. I could hear him drowning in his own blood and looking at me as if to say, "Help me."

I lifted his head and placed it in my lap. I began telling him to remain calm and tried to comfort him. I didn't have any CPR training and didn't know of anything else to do except pray for him right then and there. A few seconds later, he took his last breath. All I could think about was how I tried to stop him from kicking in that girl's door, but he was too angry to even hear me. His mother had been hurt, and he was out for blood. The paramedics and police arrived to take over and start their investigation of the crime scene. They wouldn't let anyone still in the apartment leave. I watched as they carried him out. Then, the police informed me that I had to go downtown for questioning.

We arrived at the police department, and they began questioning me about what happened, what I saw, and why I was there. I answered their questions as truthfully as I could with what little information I had. I told them exactly what I saw, minute by minute. Then, I was released. The man who shot him was picked up, released, and the charges were eventually dropped. It was ruled a justifiable homicide because of the circumstances surrounding the shooting. That was a sad no-win situation for everyone involved. Two women were fighting over a man. The brother was defending his sister by punching one of the women in the face. The son of the woman who had been punched was coming to avenge his mom's honor and was shot and killed by the same guy.

A week later, a different neighbor came to my home to inform me that the mother of the young man who was murdered wanted to talk to me, and she gave me her number. I called her. When she answered, I explained to her who I was and informed her that I had witnessed everything that happened that day. She went on to say that she knew who I was. She had heard from another witness that I prayed with her son and stayed with him while he was dying, and she just wanted to thank me for doing that. She told me I was a ram in the bush for her son that day. Because I had interceded for him in prayer that day, she believed her son went to heaven. I cried when she spoke those words. I can still hear that conversation in my head. No mother should ever have to bury her child, especially from a violent death. Seeing that man killed that day wasn't the last murder I witnessed during my crack addiction.

A couple of months after that, I was evicted for failure to pay my portion of the rent because my utilities had been turned off, and I had basically abandoned my apartment. I had completely gone past the point of no return. My mother and other family members went to clean out my apartment for me and put my furniture into a storage unit. There I was without my kids, J.D., or a place to live. I felt like giving up, but I was too afraid of taking my own life because of my fear of the Lord. Suicide was not an option. Therefore, I crawled further into the darkest places of drug addiction.

Pandora's Box Part 3

One of crack cocaine's greatest powers is stripping you of your pride. To do this, it strips you of your self-respect, dignity, morals, and values. In addition, it separates you from your relationships with family, friends, lovers, and takes away your material things. If you're a closet addict, you won't be for long because it'll force you out into the open. When you're a closet addict, you have to send other people with your money to look for and buy your crack. In doing so, you're lucky to get what you paid for, something that isn't fake, and even luckier to get anything at all.

Crack brings out the grimiest, most low down, scandalous, desperate, and dangerous sides of people. Other addicts will rob, steal, and kill you for it. Petty hustlers will sell you candle wax or just straight up take your money and dare you to stand up for yourself. When you are unable to make the money or steal it to supply the high, both female and male addicts will begin to sell themselves sexually in exchange for it.

I vividly remember the day I had reached that level of desperation. I had gone earlier to boost some things from a store and had smoked every dime I made. I had no more money nor any other resources to get more. When smoking crack, one is never enough. You just keep wanting more of it, especially if it's good quality.

I was at a crack house getting high with a female I've known for years. One of the dealers she'd normally do business with stopped by to see if there was anybody there wanting to spend some money. He looked at me and asked who I was. I was a fresh face, new on the scene, and had no money to spend. Most dealers know addiction can make women vulnerable, desperate, and willing to do whatever they want to get their fix. Although I got high, I didn't look like it. I hadn't been on the drugs long enough for it to start taking a toll on my appearance.

I've always thought of myself as being good looking. I had a nice physique, and I was always into fashion and was known for it. I didn't look or act like your stereotypical crack addict. I was still very well kept, still wearing designer clothes and shoes. I was articulate, poised, and extremely smart. He told my friend he wanted to hook up with me. He asked if I'd like to go kick it with him, and he'd make sure I was straight. That meant I could get high as much as I'd like, and he would pay me generously for my time.

I agreed. I went with him and had sex. Of course, I was nervous and didn't know what to expect or what all he expected of me for that matter. There were certain things that were totally off limits. At first, I was extremely nervous, embarrassed, and wanted to change my mind. My fear and shame left me quickly once I saw what and how much he was offering me to have sex with him.

Once we were done, he paid me with money and drugs for his time with me. I got cleaned up, and he dropped me off. We continued to do this many more times afterwards because he was generous, at least that's what I thought. That's what drug addiction and low self-esteem does to your mindset. There was nothing generous about what he'd done. I was worth so much more than that, but I had lost sight of it during that time.

I had never traded sex for drugs before in my life. That day, I learned it was easier and quicker to hustle sex or perform sexual favors than shoplifting. I could make a lot of money with fewer risk of going to jail. There are a lot of other risk one takes when trading sex. There is the risk of contracting HIV/AIDS, being beaten, going to jail, or even murdered. I took every precaution possible to avoid all of those risks. By God's grace, I came out of it fine.

Along with addiction comes a lot of disrespect, especially when you sell your body to support it. It took one incident to make me change my mind about trading sex for drugs and how I went about doing business with men during my drug addiction. I was still so very green and entirely too trusting. Those two things alone can get you messed over, taken advantage of, and even killed.

This brings me to my second time exchanging sex for drugs and money. I was walking through the projects looking to purchase some crack when I was propositioned by a guy from New Orleans. I wasn't yet familiar with all of the drug dealers from that side of town, so I assumed he was straight to deal with. I figured everything went okay with the first guy and thought this wouldn't be any different. I agreed to go with him after he made his offer, and we both made clear what we expected.

He told me he had a spot outside of the projects we could go to. He said it wasn't too far from the apartment where I was hanging out smoking dope, so he wanted to walk rather than risk driving and getting pulled over with drugs in the car. As we were walking, we passed this black girl who I recognized from one of the crack houses I frequented. I can remember how she looked at me, as if she wanted to say something. She had this terrified look on her face. I wondered, *What's wrong with her?* I looked back, and our eyes locked. Without her even saying anything verbally, her eyes said, "Don't go."

All of a sudden, I got weird vibes and discerned in my spirit that something wasn't right. I got ready to say never mind when he said, "We're almost there. Another block and we'll be there." He then began to walk towards a heavily wooded area located right behind A Dollar Store. I said, "Oh no, I'm not doing anything outside, and I'm damn sure not going in the woods with you. That's okay. I'm straight. " A fire department and a few other houses were also located there.

I tried to turn around to walk back towards the projects when he grabbed me from behind and drug me to the side of a church located right behind the Dollar Store. Then, he threatened to shoot and kill me if I didn't do what he said. I didn't know what to do. The look in his eyes was one I'll never forget. I was staring pure evil in the eyes. This was Satan himself looking at me with absolute hatred and murder in his eyes. He reached in the front of his pants like he had a gun and said, "Bitch you're going to do what I say, or I'm going to bust your ass." That meant he was going to shoot me.

I said, "Well, you're going to have to kill me, and I began screaming bloody murder at the top of my lungs. You'd have to know me or have heard me talk. My voice carries naturally. When I'm angry or excited, my voice can get extremely loud. When I began screaming, I remember hearing voices of people asking what the hell is going on. He then took off running and left me there. This was the second time in my life that I had been or was almost sexually attacked in the yard of a church. Once I thought it was safe for me to run, I ran like hell the opposite way. You'd think I would have run to the fire department, but I was afraid, in shock, and just wanted to get back to the projects.

The following day, I ran into the same girl who tried to warn me. She told me the guy who tried to attack me was one of the refugees from New Orleans, Louisiana. He had come to our area after Hurricane Katrina. He had assaulted, raped, and threatened to kill her and a few other women. I couldn't believe it. I realized just how close I had come to being raped again or murdered. I thought about how dangerous my lifestyle had become. Instead of being a sane person and stopping what I was doing, I thought of how I needed to do things differently.

> I couldn't believe it. I realized just how close I had come to being raped again or murdered.

About a week after that incident, the same guy raped and beat a white woman severely, leaving her for dead in an abandoned cemetery. The woman was found naked, badly beaten with several broken facial bones, but she survived. He was later arrested. It was also later discovered that he was in fact mentally ill and HIV positive. BUT GLORY TO GOD....HE KEPT ME AND MADE DEATH BEHAVE FOR ME !!!

After that horrifying close call, I decided to no longer hook up with the dope dealers... As if I'd be safer not dealing with them on that tip, I decided to make my money walking the streets. I started only dealing with particular men. I had a preference when it came to my clientele. They had to look a certain way, drive certain cars, be within a certain age group, and under no circumstances could they smoke crack. That would be defeating the purpose. I wasn't looking for a get high partner because I wanted all the money and drugs for myself. They had to pay me my money up front, and I would buy my own drugs. That was my sick way of trying to hold on to some sort of pride, self-respect, and dignity. It was my way of minimizing and justifying that I had basically become a prostitute. I absolutely hated the disrespect.

I hated being called a crack whore, crackhead, or junkie. I was determined to not fit in with the other females living the same lifestyle. In my mind, I wasn't any of those things. I was simply someone who enjoyed getting high. I had class. I paid for my drugs with money, and I wasn't a five-, ten-, or twenty-dollar whore. I didn't believe in pimps. There was no way I would ever sell myself and give all my money to someone else so they could live good. Again, the mindset I had was delusional. I was still giving all my money away for someone else to live good. The crack rock was my pimp, and I gave it every penny I made. In my mind, every penny I made was mine, and I made a lot of money. However, not having a pimp makes you even more vulnerable for attacks and being taken advantage of. You don't have anyone to look out for you, bail you out of jail, or school you on the do's and don'ts. I taught myself everything about street walking, and I put myself in a lot of dangerous situations and near-death experiences with complete strangers.

Looking back on those dangerous situations, I know it was NOTHING but the grace of God that kept me safe and alive. Being in the streets, you learn survival skills very quickly. I learned how to follow my discernment and intuition about people and situations. I learned how to spot potential dangers. I set rules and guidelines on how I'd conduct business with men to ensure my own safety. Whenever I'd break my own rules, I'd find myself in sticky situations. I always picked the location for us to go do our business, and if I couldn't, I wouldn't go. There could never be more than myself and the client in the car together or at the picked location. I would always have them roll their window down completely, so I could reach into the car to open the door from the inside, just to make sure the doors weren't trap doors. Finally, I'd always ask, "Are you the police or affiliated with the police in any way?" That was just in case it was a prostitution sting or something.

I never discussed exchanging sexual favors for money. I was just simply looking to have a good time with someone who wanted to have a good time as well. Then, I'd say, "But I am looking for a donation of (whatever I wanted) to go towards me finding shelter and food." Those rules I set were important for my safety and survival. Each time I broke one, something would happen to remind me as to why I had set them in the first place. Even taking safety precautions, setting rules for yourself to go by, and setting boundaries, there was always that chance of something going horribly wrong.

When you're living that lifestyle, and you have loyal, frequent clients, many times they will get comfortable with you and will only deal with you. You build a rapport with them and get to know them a little better. However, you never really know the real person you're dealing with because you only see them when they want sex. You only know the representative, the one they appear or pretend to be when they're around you. When dealing with regular clients, you have to be careful as not to become emotionally involved with them. You don't discuss personal and intimate details about your life, where you live, or anything that could make them feel as if it's more between you than just business.

I tried everything I could think of to ensure my safety, health, and my freedom. But I let my guard down a little with this one client, and it later proved how dangerous letting your guard down could be. I didn't have my own place. I was staying in motels, in crack houses, and with relatives from time to time. There was an empty duplex where I'd had been staying on nights when it was hot from police activity. I would stay there if I wanted to get high alone, because of bad weather, or if I just wanted some uninterrupted sleep. I had this frequent customer I'll call Marvin. I'd been seeing him for a while. On occasion, he had driven by that duplex and saw me either entering or exiting it. He'd blow or even sometimes stop to say a few words. I didn't think anything of it. Surely, he didn't think I was staying there.

One night, I got a call from another regular client of mine who was in town for a business conference. He'd always call my cell phone whenever he got to town to let me know he was here. He'd ask if he could see me. On this particular night, my client asked if I had a spot we could go to, and he'd give me extra money if I could find a place that was safe. We didn't have time to go back to the hotel where he was going to be staying. Besides that, his business partners were all staying at the same hotel. Of course, it would look awkward if he returned to the hotel with me, considering he wasn't from Knoxville.

I took him to the abandoned apartment I'd been staying in from time to time. I had candles, a kerosene heater, a blow-up mattress and other things I had purchased for my survival. We walked in the duplex. I did my walk through to make sure nobody else had entered while I was gone, and we proceeded on with our business as usual. When he was finished, he left. Just as I was about to get dressed to go shower at a relative's, I heard someone say my name. Remember, this duplex was abandoned. It wasn't run down or anything like that. It was simply vacant and had no utilities whatsoever.

When I heard my name called, it nearly scared me to death. I yelled, "Who is that?" I grabbed a candle and proceeded cautiously to where I heard the voice coming from but not near enough for them to grab me.

Again, I yelled, "Who is that?"

"It's me, Marvin," the voice replied.

Remember the client I said had driven by and saw me going in or out of the duplex on a few occasions. It was him. He had entered the duplex that night when I went to meet my other client from out of town, waited on me, and was hiding in a closet the entire time, listening to me having sex. It freaked me out. All kinds of thoughts began running through my head.

He's stalking me. He could kill me and get away with it. He could've killed me and my other client, and nobody would've ever known the truth.

Once the initial shock wore off, I became furious with him. I didn't let him know it because I was afraid of what he might do. If he'd go to that extreme, be bold enough to enter without permission and sit and listen to me having sex, he was capable of anything. I played it off and told him my cousin was picking me up at any moment, so I could go shower. I instructed him to meet me back there in an hour. I never returned to that duplex, nor did I deal with him ever again after that stunt. That was too creepy for me. I realized he had become emotionally invested in me, and I didn't trust him anymore.

Pandora's Box Part 4

It was a beautiful day outside, lots of traffic, and potential clients were riding around looking for a date. A small, grey pickup truck pulled into a parking lot and motioned for me. I had been up for a couple of days straight, and I was tired.... So, my judgement and observation were off. I approached the car and motioned for him to lower his window. He was a good looking, clean cut, younger white male. We greeted one another and both agreed to my terms. I reached inside to open the door, and I got in.

After we had been riding and talking for a few minutes, I begin giving him specific directions on where to turn, and he kept passing them up. At first, I thought he was just nervous and wanted to make sure I wasn't a danger to him, or maybe he was an undercover officer, so I didn't allow myself to become alarmed. I did become alarmed at a certain point. He kept ignoring my directions and looking in his rear-view mirror. I thought, *I believe he's undercover law enforcement and I need to wiggle my way out of this.* I hadn't said anything incriminating, so I told him I changed my mind and asked him to pull over so I could get out.

He ignored me yet again, and I could feel him accelerate his speed. I was looking in the mirrors to see behind us. I was checking to see if we were being followed. Then, I heard a voice say, "If you stay in this truck with him, you're going to be his first victim." I immediately looked over at him, and I saw a demonic force all over his face. His eyes were dark, hollow, and evil.

> Then, I heard a voice say, "If you stay in this truck with him, you're going to be his first victim."

I then said, "You aren't crazy, are you?" He looked at me and smirked.

I said, "Okay, pull over right now and let me out of this truck right now!"

I began reaching for the door handle when he said with a calm and comforting voice, "Wait a minute, baby, I'm not going to hurt you. This is my first time ever doing this, and I'm just as scared as you are. Here's the money right here. Go ahead and put it in your purse if it makes you feel better. If everything goes smoothly, I'll come see you regularly."

I counted the money, put it in my purse, and totally

ignored the warning bells roaring in my spirit and gut.

He then said, "I'd rather go to a place that's a little safer for both of us. I promise you nothing will happen that you don't want to happen, and I'll bring you right back." Before I knew it, we were in the next county, and he seemed to become obviously anxious and more suspicious to me. Something was off and very much wrong. The presence of danger and evil were overwhelming. He kept looking into his mirror, so I looked again to see what he was looking at. Suddenly, another truck that had been behind us for quite some time came around and made a right-hand turn.

The guy said, "Do see where that truck turned? That's where we're going."

My mouth fell open, and I couldn't believe where he was pulling up to. It was a funeral home. There were no other vehicles in the parking lot, and it was still broad daylight outside.

I replied, "What the hell are you doing, and why are we at a funeral home?"

He pulled to the back of the building and parked close to one of the doors. I thought, *Either he works for this funeral home, or whoever was driving the other truck works here. Perhaps it's a family-owned funeral home.* Speaking of other trucks, I didn't see the one that had just turned into the parking lot before us. I believe it had pulled into a tent located out back because I never saw it again. The guy kept trying to get me to come inside, and I refused. "I'm not going in there, hell no!"

I noticed he kept looking up towards a heavily wooded area behind the funeral home and started trying to get me to go into the woods. That is when he reached for me, and we started struggling. I began digging into my purse for anything to fight him off and could only find an ink pen. I pretended it was a weapon, and I threatened him, which seemed to only infuriate him even more. I remembered the door worked, so I reached for the handle. I fought him off me and jumped out screaming and hollering at the top of my lungs. There was a grocery store and a car wash located in a shopping plaza to the right of the funeral home. I saw a Hispanic male at the carwash and ran to him screaming, "Please help me." He didn't speak very good English but was able to understand enough to help me.

The Hispanic guy agreed to give me ride back to town. Once I was inside his truck, the adrenaline and realization of what almost happened sent me into a meltdown. I was trembling uncontrollably and thanking the man for helping me. I should've been thanking God. Once again, GLORY TO GOD! HE KEPT ME AND MADE DEATH BEHAVE FOR ME AGAIN!!

Pandora's Box Part 5

After already having a couple of close calls, one would think it would've been enough to deter anyone from continuing to live such a dangerous and unpredictable lifestyle. Sadly, it wasn't. I continued to put myself in compromising and unsafe predicaments. After those close calls, I tried to be more selective and even more cautious of who I dealt with. However, danger isn't always seen or easily detected. Drugs create monsters out of people. They become masters at disguising and fooling people enough to get them comfortable with them. Then, by the time you discover who they truly are and what their true intentions are, many times it's too late.

I was out on one of my walks looking to make some money. It was still summertime. On this day, I noticed a shiny pretty, fiery red Cadillac with a drive out tag. It had been circling the block for quite some time. After passing me a few times already, I guess he built up the courage and decided to stop, pull over, and motion for me. I thought, *He's new.* I had never seen him or his car in the area before. He was a very handsome black guy, around my age. He appeared to have a little money. I approached the car, and he told me to get in.

Right away he flashed cash, a Ziploc baggy full of crack rocks, and said he was just looking for someone to have a good time with. One of my rules had always been not to do business with anyone who got high. He went on to justify and explain that he did not do it all the time. He explained he made too much money to be hooked on crack. That was just one of those days that he wanted to chill with a beautiful young lady and get high.

This day, I broke that rule and decided to go with him. He was very well dressed, driving a nice car, and had plenty of drugs and money. He wasn't your typical crack smoker. We ended up going to an apartment not too far from the projects. It was very nice, well-kept, and still in the hood. That was where he told me he made most of his money. We went inside and began to smoke dope. We talked and listened to some music, and I was really feeling comfortable with him until he started fidgeting. I figured it was a side effect from the dope. To keep him from blowing my buzz, I scooted off the couch and sat on the floor to continue getting high.

We had been in the apartment for well over an hour. He hadn't said or done anything to arouse my suspicion, so I continued getting high. As I was sitting there, I could see him get more nervous and start fidgeting even more. I blew it off because I thought it was just his trip when he got high. Yet, out of my peripheral vision, I saw him reach inside his pants, but he had done that several times. The last time he did it, a voice told me to get up off the floor. I attempted to ignore it and continue smoking the dope until the voice spoke again. With an urgency, the voice said, "Get up off of the floor right now!"

As soon as I got up and sat on the couch, there was a loud bang! I smelled gun powder and literally saw smoke coming from inside his pants. I realized the man had shot himself straight through his leg, and the bullet landed exactly in the spot where I had been sitting for at least an hour. That was the first time I realized he even had a gun. I looked at the bullet hole in the floor and asked, "What the hell are you doing?"

He responded, "Damn, I just shot myself. I need to go to the hospital." Of course, I jumped up and started gathering my things together when he said, "You've got to drive me to the hospital."

I knew that they'd call the police because it was a shooting, and they'd have some questions. Before getting in the car, he placed the gun he'd shot himself with in the trunk and covered it with some stuff he had in there. I didn't want to be caught in the middle of that, so I tried to figure a way out of the whole mess. I drove him to the hospital. He told me he was going to tell them that someone else shot him and for me to go along with everything he said.

Once we arrived at the hospital, he told the emergency room staff that someone else had shot him, and they called the police. As soon as they took him to the back for treatment, I told them I was going to park the car in a proper parking space. My fear got the best of me. I had a warrant on me for failure to appear in court for child support. I knew if they ran my name I was going to jail. I didn't want to be caught up in that freak accident, so instead of parking and returning inside, I left the hospital in his car. My intentions were to drive the car back to those apartments, put his keys under the mat, and leave it there for him to find when he got out of the hospital.

I drove around for a minute trying to collect my thoughts about what to do. I didn't want anything to happen to the man's car, so I was trying to figure out what I should do with it. About two hours had passed. Then, all of a sudden, I was surrounded by police cars. It was like a scene out of a movie. They jumped out yelling with their guns drawn. That man told the police I stole his car, and he believed I set the whole thing up. At that point, I felt I had no choice but to tell them the whole story about how we met, what we had been doing when he shot himself, and whose idea it was to lie about it. They ordered me out of the car, placed me in handcuffs, put me in the police car, and began questioning me.

Of course, I told them everything, agreed to show them where the apartment was, and told them where they could find the gun. After searching the trunk of the car, they impounded it. They asked for my driver's license. Of course, I didn't have one. I explained I was only driving to get him to the hospital because he'd shot himself. I gave them a false name, date of birth, and social security number. After they ran the information, I was released. I had never walked so fast in my life to get away from them. I prayed, "Lord, please don't let them come back looking for me or figure out I was using a false identity." I don't know whatever happened to that guy or whatever came of that situation. I never saw him or that Cadillac again.

Once again, God had protected me from another dangerous situation. The more I thought about and played the events back in my head I realize how dangerous it was. So many thoughts and questions came to my mind, *Was he actually planning on shooting me in the back of the head and leaving me there or what?* I could've been shot in the neck or back. I could've been paralyzed or worse, dead. TO GOD BE THE GLORY YET AGAIN, FOR HIS GRACE AND MERCY!

Pandora's Box Part 6

Not much time went by after that before I found myself in trouble again. I was running through an abandoned graveyard in the projects screaming for my life. An old, beat-up pick-up truck pulled alongside me. Inside the truck was an older white guy. As I approached the truck, he began to speak. I could tell by his voice and how he pronounced his words that the man was deaf. I reached inside the truck and opened it from the inside so I could get in. There were no interior lights, and I immediately started trying to communicate with him. We couldn't understand each other, so I immediately changed my mind and motioned for him to pull the truck over so I could get out. At that moment, he committed the first violation. He flicked a lighter and hit a crack pipe. The light from the lighter allowed me to see the wild and empty look in his eyes. He kept driving, and I was reminded that he couldn't hear me.

Suddenly, I could feel his hand frantically moving around in the seat under some garments I was sitting on. I asked him what he was doing. I reached inside my purse to find a lighter, so I could see what he was reaching for. As soon as I flicked on the lighter, he pulled a machete from beneath me. I opened the door of the truck when he got to the cemetery and jumped out while it was still moving. I ran through the abandoned cemetery that runs through the projects where I hung out. I screamed for help. GLORY TO GOD FOR SAVING ME AGAIN!

At that moment, I knew I had to do things differently before I ran out of chances.

One weekend, I was in a abandoned apartment getting high when I heard a round of gunfire. With that many shots, I knew someone was either dead or had been shot multiple times. I walked to the door, looked out, and saw my cousin David running through the projects towards the area where the shooting had occurred. The area he was running toward was the area where my uncle Curtis hung out and sold drugs. My heart sank. I yelled David's name and asked, "David is that Curtis?"

He replied, "Yea" and kept running.

I ran out the door towards where David had run. When I got there, I could see people huddled around my uncle's lifeless body lying on the ground.

I asked, "Is he dead?" They said yes. I lost it and belted out the loudest scream I've ever let out in my life. After I calmed down enough to even think clearly, I called my mom to tell her. Somebody had already made the call. My mom, my aunt Connie, and other relatives showed up. The police had the area sealed off and were doing their routine investigation. It took hours before they even picked him up off the ground. I watched in disbelief as they loaded him into the coroner's van. There was no arrest, no suspects, and no witnesses! Everyone knows that in the projects, there's always a witness or several, but people will not come forward for whatever reasons.

> I was in the abandoned apartment getting high when I heard a round of gunfire.

After my uncle Curtis was murdered, I became more and more angry as the days went by. Not one person was willing to at least make an anonymous call with information leading to an arrest. My uncle Curtis sold drugs, but he also gave back to that community. All year round, he'd collect things like clothes, perfumes, colognes, and toys. Anything a shoplifter brought him, he purchased it. At Christmas time, he'd open the trunk of his car and pass out wrapped gifts to anybody and everybody. On Mother's Day, he'd do the same thing.

I know selling crack is wrong, and it's poison, but my uncle Curtis was a different kind of drug dealer. He looked out for people, bought them food, took the less fortunate kids from the projects to the fair when it came to town, and had huge fireworks show for the community on July 4. He even hosted Easter egg hunts where he'd hide $100 bills in eggs. Crack smokers could go to him with $2.00, and he'd give them something just to keep them from feening for it. Understand this, in no way am I making him out to be some kind of hero for enabling people's addiction or capitalizing from it. I'm simply saying he was one of the good guys who found the wrong kind of hustle to make money.

A couple days prior to my uncle Curtis' funeral, I went on a war path about nobody in that community coming forward. "My uncle put groceries in your refrigerators, and not one of you is willing to speak up." That's what I was yelling, along with a few expletives, as I walked through the projects drunk. As I walked the outskirts of the projects continuing my rant, the police rode by and saw that I was drunk and belligerent, so they pulled over and approached me. They asked me my name and DOB. I was out of control at this point because I knew I was going to jail. They ran my name, and sure enough, I had outstanding warrants for child support and failure to appear in court.

As one officer tried to handcuff me, I started resisting and fighting. Another officer ran from across the street and clotheslined me. That almost set off World War III. I became uncontrollably angry and told the officers they were going to have to kill me. It took several of them to get me cuffed and restrained, and I only weighed

165lbs at the most. I remember my mother pulling up after she had been called and told I was being arrested. They asked her if I was mentally ill or on some sort of medication because of the strength I had during their tussle with me. They said they'd never encountered a woman so physically strong.

At times, we have laughed about that comment the police made that night. But it sure wasn't funny then. I had a hold on me and no bail, so I didn't get to go to my uncle's funeral. I had to grieve his death in jail, and I stayed in there for about 60 days before I was released. I didn't want to go back to those projects anymore, but I wasn't done with that phase of my life, so I changed the location where I hung out.

One night while walking through another high crime heavy drug infested neighborhood in East Knoxville, a black guy in an SUV approached me and called me to his truck. I had never seen him a day in my life and vice versa. I walked over, and he asked my name. I told him. Then I asked what or who was he looking for? At that moment, he looked at me with a serious, curious, yet concerned look and said, "What are you doing out here? You don't belong out here. You're different, and I can tell that simply by how articulately you speak!" He then identified himself as an undercover cop and showed me his badge.

He said, "Tameka, get off these streets. You are out of place. You do not belong out here. You stick out like a sore thumb, and I don't want to see you back out here anymore. If I do, I'm arresting you for your own good."

I was relieved that he didn't take me to jail and felt good he could see past my brokenness and my addiction. He could also tell I was different from a lot of the others. Looking back, I truly believe God put him in that place that night. He wanted to stop me from who knows what kind of danger or trouble awaiting me. Not even two days later, a similar encounter happened again.

I got in the car with a middle-aged black gentleman. As we began to talk, he looked at me and asked, "What are you doing out here? You don't belong out here? Listen to how well and proper you speak!"

He handed me a hand full of cash, pulled over immediately, and told me to be safe and get off the streets. Knoxville isn't that big of a city, and I never saw either of those men again! I ended up being arrested again some months later. This time, I was court ordered to treatment. I got kicked out of the first treatment facility, and I voluntarily walked out of the second one. But I was tired of running, tired of getting high, tired of living that life, just sick and tired of being sick and tired. So, I ended up going to sign up for Section 8 housing to get me a place to stay at least, and my lawyer got me into mental health therapy to keep me out of jail. I soon got my apartment again and was diagnosed through therapy with post-traumatic stress disorder, which qualified me for disability. I was no longer walking the streets, selling my body, or putting myself in dangerous situations, and by The Grace of God, I did not have a criminal record. Well, I didn't have any felonies at least. I only had an arrest for disorderly conduct, drug paraphernalia, failure to appear, and child support but no felonies or prostitution charges. Glory to God.

From the Crack House to God's House

CHAPTER 11

Right before I got approved for Section 8 housing, I met Mr. Larry. He was a retired 73-year-old white man who was divorced, had no children, and was lonely. I believe Mr. Larry took to me for two reasons. He was lonely, and I think he felt sorry for me. He was so free hearted and would always come looking for me to bring me money and food, even taking me to his house and giving me my own room, so I'd have a place to stay whenever I needed. Mr. Larry did a lot for me. He bought me clothes, a car, and even paid off my child support arrears of $30,000 to prevent me from going back to jail. He was truly a blessing to me in so many ways, but he was also an enabler and toxic for me.

Mr. Larry would give me money to buy crack and smoke it at his house. He said he'd rather me be there than to be out on the streets doing it. Mr. Larry had become attached, possessive, and he used his money and my addiction to control me. I believe it gave him a sense of power to feel needed.

I eventually got approved for Section 8 housing and was able to get my own place. Mr. Larry furnished it for me and eventually bought me a car too, so I would have transportation to look for employment and get wherever I needed to go. I would find jobs and work a week or two. Then, I would quit because my addiction wouldn't let me hold a steady job. Mr. Larry would fuss about me asking him for money to get high, yet he'd give it to me anyway. There were times he'd sit right in my living room, hand me his ATM card, and allow me to go back and forth to the ATM to withdraw money to buy crack. Then, there were days I'd literally have to beg him for money to get high. I believe he got a kick out of it. Me begging him somehow fed his desire to feel needed, and it empowered him. This went on for at least 4 years.

One day, I made the decision to go to a rehab facility out of town. Mr. Larry drove me there and would visit me a couple of times during my 30 days of treatment, but deep down I knew as long as Mr. Larry was in my life, he'd be a trigger for me because I knew he had plenty of money and I could manipulate him into giving me as much as I wanted. So, after 30 days of treatment, I was released and returned home. That same evening, I had a crack pipe in my hand.

As time went on, Mr. Larry would begin to criticize me for my addiction, and he'd punish me by not coming around for a day. Then, he'd show up and would be super friendly and sweet. During those times, I knew I could ask him for drug money, and he'd say yes with no hesitations. Then, one time, we had a disagreement about me getting high, and I said to him, "But you're the one who buys it for me!" He left and didn't come by for 2 or 3 days. When he popped back up, he sat around for at least an hour almost as if he was waiting for something.

> ...he had in fact been sitting there wanting me to ask him because he came prepared.

Mr. Larry had become a trigger for me. Of course, my crack cravings flared up, so I sweet talked him and asked him if he'd just buy me one? Just one, that's all I needed to get rid of the craving. He then responded, "No sweetheart, you're doing good, don't do that." I was shocked, so I repeatedly asked him, and he repeatedly said no, even pretending like he was going to leave until I started begging him to stay.

He then said, "Hold on, let me go to the car."

When he returned, he had a brown paper bag with him. Inside of the bag were my brand of cigarettes, brand new brillo, a brand-new rose glass pipe, and brand new lighter. I realized he had already anticipated me asking, and he had in fact been sitting there wanting me to ask him because he came prepared. That scenario repeated itself over and over. At one point, he would no longer have to walk back to his car to get the paraphernalia he bought me. He'd have it on him already, in his pockets. He'd only pull it out after I would have asked 5 or 6 times and he had said no. In that moment, I stopped being in denial and accepted that this was a very unhealthy friendship for me, and if I had any hopes of recovering, I needed to get out of it because that was codependency on both of our parts.

I again tried to seek recovery, this time through an outpatient facility. I remember telling my therapist and sharing with the group about my friendship with Mr. Larry. My therapist told me Mr. Larry was a narcissist, and I'd better prepare myself for him to leave once I got clean. She told me Mr. Larry would discard me and find someone else with an addictive personality to control. He was fond of my mother, and Mama, along with other relatives, had taken a liking to him as well. They knew about all of the wonderful ways he'd had a positive impact on my life and how he'd helped me so much financially.

My mother was in Nashville to have a surgical procedure done, and Mr. Larry drove me there to be with her. The surgery was a success, so we thought. We waited until she came out of recovery. When they brought her out, I was so happy to see her. However, as her daughter, I could tell something was off. I couldn't explain it, but she didn't look right in her face or as she had the other times coming out of the same surgery. Once she was put in her room and about to rest, I hugged, kissed, and told her we were going back to Knoxville and asked her to call me after she rested. Upon returning to Knoxville that night, I started getting high, again.

About an hour into it, I got a call from my stepdad telling me that my mother had to be rushed back into emergency surgery and was now in ICU. I started screaming and crying, asking all kinds of questions, "What happened, she was fine when we left?" After hanging up with him, I was immediately consumed with guilt. My mother didn't look right to me when she came out of surgery that morning, and I said nothing. If I had spoken up, maybe she wouldn't have been in ICU. I was entirely too high to have Mr. Larry drive me right back down that highway. It was extremely late, and it was a three-hour drive. I remember begging God to keep my mother alive and let me get back to Nashville to see what was going on. I wanted to find out what the hell happened after we left.

I didn't get high anymore that night nor did I go to sleep. As soon as the sun came up, we were back on the highway headed to Nashville. Nothing could've prepared me for what I was about to see walking into my mother's ICU room. She was in an induced coma, on a breathing machine, and there were IV'S and tubes everywhere. The doctor tried to prepare me before opening the door to her room, but he couldn't. When I saw her, I broke down screaming and remember looking at the Black doctor. I asked, "What have y'all done? Y'all have to fix this. Please fix this. I need my mama."

The hospital she was in is also a teaching hospital where interns (who are wanting to be surgeons) are allowed to operate on patients. The doctor told us an intern had made a mistake surgically and that was what caused her issues. I was in disbelief, *Not my mommy God.*

They left me in the room alone with her for a few minutes, and I prayed and begged God to spare my mommy, to allow me the opportunity to get clean, get myself all the way together, and allow her to be here to see it. I then kissed her, held her hand, and told how sorry I was for everything I'd ever put her through. I told her I needed her to fight and get better. Whew, this made me tear up all over again just thinking about that moment. *I love my mother so much!*

To God be the glory.... They were able to correct the issue, and my mom came home and is in good health.

I went without getting high for a few weeks after that incident, but that old demon wasn't through fighting me yet. I had a neighbor whose boyfriend sold crack, and he was having car problems at the time. He propositioned me to use my car by paying me with crack. I thought to myself, *That might be easier to do than to have to go through the whole begging game with Mr. Larry,* so I agreed. Pawning my car out to my neighbor's boyfriend became a new way for me to get high, so this went on for about two months. Then, on July 4, 2015, I had been up on a five-day crack binge, and my neighbor's boyfriend had my car. He'd had it all week, and that's how I managed to be up for five days smoking crack. No sleep, no eating, just getting high.

I was sitting at my dining room table when my cell phone rang. I answered. On the other end, I heard GOD speaking directly to me through Minister Saundra Phillips. I had not seen nor talked to her in years. She had gotten my number from my mom because she said God had given her a message for me.

> Nothing had ever shaken me more than that phone call.

Her first words were, "GOD TOLD ME TO TELL YOU YOUR NEXT BLOW COULD BE YOUR LAST ONE."

She then went on to say, "You're your mother's only daughter. Don't let her find you dead that way.

Out of all the close calls and near-death experiences, the people who tried to encourage me to get off of the streets, the nights in jail, the failed rehab stays, the NA and AA meetings, seeing the hurt I had caused my own babies, and those that loved me, *nothing had ever shaken me more than that phone call*. It was different. It wasn't Minister Saundra I heard over the phone that day. It was GOD HIMSELF.

After we finished talking on the phone, I hung up and sat there for a minute. I heard The Holy Spirit say to me, "You can quit getting high and live, or you can keep getting high and die. The choice is yours." It was a voice so clear, powerful, yet gentle and straight forward. I picked up my cell phone, called my neighbor's boyfriend, told him to bring me my car, and I was done. He said and offered me everything to let him keep the car another day. But I said, "No, I'm done."

I'm sure he didn't believe me. I'm sure he had heard that a million times from other customers. He came to the house and dropped the hardest crack rock I'd ever heard or seen since I'd been getting high throughout the years, but I was done, and I meant it. He gave me back my car keys and left. I went to bed that night, and I think I may have slept for two whole days from being up on a five-day crack binge. I got up that day and began to clean my bedroom. As I was moving a clothes basket from my bedroom closet, a crack pipe fell out of it and landed on the very top of my foot. I looked down and realized it was the crack pipe I had hidden from myself during that five-day binge and was entirely too high to find it. I reached down to pick it up, and my mouth literally watered because it was still loaded and packed with crack residue inside of the glass. It was probably enough residue in that glass pipe to scrape out and recook a good $30 piece, at the least.

My mouth had never watered before for anything, but it did when I picked up that pipe. In that moment, I could see into the spiritual realm. I was being tempted by Satan himself. I remember hearing the Holy Spirit tell me to step on it and crush it. I walked out onto my balcony, and I stomped it until it was just tiny particles of glass. I could literally feel GOD breaking the chains off me and setting me free from crack addiction.

I went to church that following Sunday at Kingdom Life with Bishop Gary Wright and First Lady Frenchie Wright. They were there to welcome me in with open arms and hearts. I never looked back. **God is so good that I didn't have one single craving, desire, or taste for it ever again!**

When I got to Kingdom Life that Sunday, I had an uncontrollable praise down deep inside of me. I jumped up and down, crying and rejoicing that God had delivered me. I knew people were worried, doubtful, and I'm willing to bet some of them betted on me relapsing. OH, BUT WHOMEVER GOD SETS FREE, IS FREE INDEED.

I continued busting the church doors down every Sunday, and I eventually joined Kingdom Life. I soon went back to school to get my GED after dropping out in the 10th grade. Mind you, I was in my late 30's to early 40's by this time. I hadn't been to school in years, and I scored college level on everything, except math, but I passed it. I've always hated math but always had a love for English, science, and reading. I got a scholarship to go to a community college, and I enrolled in Pellissippi to study to be a paralegal. I got bored with that really fast and decided to put that on hold.

Immediately after that, my daughter had gotten into some trouble, and I had to get temporary custody of her two girls while she got that worked out and she eventually did. I had the girls about two months. Then, they went back to live with their wonderful mother. As believers, we know the enemy is always plotting and planning attacks to destroy us. He couldn't take me out with all the other attacks and adversities. He knew he had to become a little more clever and conceal himself even more in order to attack me now. I had gotten stronger, my spiritual eyes had been opened, he knew he couldn't use drugs as a weapon to attempt to destroy me anymore, so it wouldn't be long after my grandbabies went back home that I'd find myself in more spiritual warfare.

As for Mr. Larry, eventually he stopped coming around as much. In fact, the only time he'd come around was for Thanksgiving dinner at my mom's. She'd invite him every year because she knew he was an elderly man who lived alone. Sadly, two years ago, Mr. Larry committed suicide by hanging himself. His ex-wife came to my job to deliver the news because she knew we had been close at one time. She brought me a card that she'd found in his house. He had addressed it to me. I opened and it read. *I am so proud of you. Love your friend, Larry.* He left money inside of the envelope. It tore me up, and I went into the bathroom at work and cried my eyes out. I was so upset that my supervisor thought it'd be best if I went home for the rest of the day to deal with my grief. I often think of him and all of the positive things he did for me. I smile and say, "Thank you, old friend, for everything. I will forever remember your kind heart!"

The Spirit of Jezebel

CHAPTER 12

As you grow in your walk with God, the more intense the devil's attacks will be and the more creative he must be with his attacks on you. Without studying and knowing God's word, you're more susceptible to schemes and attacks of the enemy. Satan has many demons and spirits, but one of the most powerful, strongest, and more demonic of these spirits is the Jezebel spirit.

I truly believe I became influenced by the spirit of Jezebel through my years of being sexually active and promiscuous. At the time, I didn't realize it and couldn't identify with it because I hadn't heard of it nor was I in the Word of God to study and learn about it. It wasn't until years later that I learned of it. The Jezebel spirit is very cunning and seductive. It is responsible for destroying marriages, causing people to commit murder, or even suicide. It refuses to admit guilt or wrong! The spirit of Jezebel uses people to accomplish its agenda. This spirit withholds information, lies, criticizes, sows seeds of discord, uses the element of surprise, is vengeful, and so much more.

Here's what happened and how I overcame it. I had been sexually dealing with a man who was married for years. It started during my prostitution days and continued, even after I had gotten delivered from drugs. We all know that sex can be extremely powerful in bonding two people. That is why God created sex for a husband and a wife. He calls it fornication when you have sex without being married. During the entire time I was sleeping with this man (while on drugs), I never had any emotional attachment to him.

It wasn't until I stopped getting high that my feelings for him developed. I later realized that being involved with him from the very start was demonic. I will never forget this particular demonic experience. One day, we were at my house and had just finished being intimate. My bedroom was directly across from the bathroom. As I got up to go to the bathroom, I was looking in the mirror, and I saw this indescribable dark force with lightning speed run right past the mirror. It was behind me. *I was not imagining this. I had not been drinking, and I was completely sober.*

This spirit ran fast, and it was dark and evil looking. I jumped and turned around saying, "What the hell?" This man was smiling within arm's reach. I asked the guy I was seeing if he saw it. He smiled and said, "Saw what?" That shook me to my core because I knew what I'd just saw, but I couldn't make sense of it. I knew that something evil and demonic was present, but I blew it off.

I was delusional, vulnerable, naive, gullible, and.....

Although I couldn't forget it, I ignored that encounter and continued seeing him anyway. We even started talking more intimately. He would confide in me about the problems in his marriage and how unhappy he was. As time went on, he and I started talking about him leaving her and coming to be with me. I was delusional, vulnerable, naive, gullible, and was being used for his sexual gratification. The more he told me about their tumultuous marriage the more I got attached to him, and the more I was willing to do for him. If I was willing to do what she wasn't doing, he'd definitely leave her for me, at least that's what I thought.

Of course, that wasn't all in my head. He encouraged those thoughts and feelings. One time, he even had me to look for a different location for us to move together. This would be out of the way and would make our transition of moving in together easier. Another way he manipulated me was by telling me how lazy his wife was and how everything was always on him financially. As time went on, I started giving him money to help him get back on his feet. I would also buy him material things, thinking that would make him love and want me more and help speed up the process. However, there was always an excuse as to why it wasn't happening and why he needed more time. The longer it took, the more I gave. The more I did, the more anxious I became and the more dangerous the whole situation got.

I would get angry with him when he couldn't answer my calls, text me back, or get away to come see me. Of course, he'd always calm my mind by feeding me some bull crap to pacify me for the time being. The holidays were the absolute worst, but they began to open my eyes up to the reality of things. One Valentine's day, he showed up to my house with candy, flowers, balloons, and a card. I felt special, loved, and convinced that this man was going to be with me in the end. But leave it up to good ole Facebook to give you a reality check.

His wife had posted pictures of the gifts he had gotten her. There was a video of him in the mall at a jewelry store picking out a bracelet. Then, there was another one of him in an expensive designer bags store. He was buying her a purse. I thought to myself, *This doesn't look like a man who is ready to leave his wife. This man is stringing you along and is neglecting you at the same time.*

I will never forget how cheap and played I felt in that moment, and you'd think it was enough to wake me up and cause me to walk away. Nope! Not me, I was determined to win this man. I became more competitive in every area: in the bedroom, with my gifts, my attention, my affection, and my love. I was absolutely delusional when it came to him. I let him have his way with me sexually, financially, emotionally, and mentally.

In the midst of this insanity, one of my paternal brothers and I had reunited after years of not seeing each other. We went out to have lunch one day, and we got on the topic of making money. He told me he had weight in weed if I knew anyone looking. He said he'd front me some to sell to make me some money if I wanted it. I instantly thought of "Him" because that's what he did, hustled weed. So, I told my brother about him. I said he would get rid of it faster and better than I could. I asked if he'd be willing to help me out by fronting it to him instead.

I set up the meeting between the two of them, and a business agreement was made between us all. I had been knowing of this dude for years and had never heard about any grimy stuff on his part. I was sleeping with him, and I truly thought he genuinely cared for me.

Everything went smoothly the first couple of times my brother fronted him. He got rid of the weed, made the money, and my brother got his. It wasn't until my brother fronted him a larger amount that he did the unthinkable. After my brother fronted him a large quantity of weed, he expected to hear from him in a certain amount of time. When that time came, he heard nothing from him. He got all of that weed and decided to forget me and my brother. He just kept the money. My brother was livid, and he unfortunately believed I was in on it. That broke my heart that he would think I'd knowingly introduce him to someone so dishonest and lowdown. That goes to show you the mindset I had at that time. It was horrible!

If he could betray his wife the way he had, I should've known it was nothing for him to betray me and my brother. My brother and I ended up falling out, and some things were said on both of our parts that should never be said between siblings. At this point, I was realizing this dude didn't care anything about me. He was only using me. I got in my car and went looking for "him." I was hurt, angry, and embarrassed that he made me look like a liar and a fool to my brother. There was absolutely nothing I could say to my brother to convince him I had no idea and no part in what "he" had done.

I pulled up on him at a gas station not too far from his house. He had his young son with him. There were other people in and outside of the store, but I did not care. I was beyond the point of no return. I went into a rage! I walked into the store, swinging and cussing, "Where's the money?" This dude was like 6'3, about 200 plus pounds, and I did not care. As I was swinging on him and cursing, he looked at me as if he wanted to hit me back, and I dared him. I told him I wished he would, so I could stab him to death right there. The owner of the store, along with other customers, talked me down and helped defuse the situation. He walked out of store, got in his car, and left. I kept trying to call him and give him time to bring me the money, but he never did.

We stopped seeing each other for a while after that, but as time went by, he started coming back around. I know what you're thinking, *That should've been it.* No, I shouldn't have ever dealt with him again. However, when you're not in God's will, it's not easy to fight off spirits, especially the Jezebel spirit. He had this believable and convincing excuse as to what happened with the money. He said he entrusted someone else to help him get the weed off, and they claimed they were robbed, so he promised to make it right with my brother as soon as he got the chance. I believed him, and we picked up right where we'd left off.

I told him how hard it was for me to leave him alone, and he jokingly told me I wouldn't be able to because he'd buried a pair of my panties in the ground somewhere. That made me feel uneasy to hear. I asked him where he learned about witchcraft. I think he said he learned from his grandmother. I can't exactly remember verbatim, but I do recall him saying he learned it as a younger man in his home state up north. I again brushed it off, and we continued our affair. Things between us became even more demonic, violent, and dangerous.

One evening while his wife was out of town, we made plans for that night, and he was supposed to be coming to see me. When the time came, I called him and got no answer. I texted, and he responded that he was at home and couldn't leave or talk because his stepson was there. That didn't sit right with me, and I got the sudden urge to drive by his house. My instincts were telling me he was lying, and he wasn't at home. He was somewhere else with another female.

I pulled in his driveway and sure enough his car was gone. That sent me into another rage. I circled the block repeatedly for over an hour, calling and got no answer. The last time I circled around to go back to his house, he was getting out of his car. I called his phone and asked where he'd been. I asked what happened to our plans and him coming to my house?. He tried to rush me off the phone and pretended someone was in the house and would hear us talking.

I said, "Either you come out to meet me somewhere for us to talk, or I am going to destroy your car." I knew him. He would lie to get away from his wife and come see me. In my heart, I knew he had pulled the same stunt on me.

He said, "If you touch my car, I am going to start shooting."

I replied, "Well, get to shooting got damn it!"

I threw my car into park, got a hammer out of my trunk, and I broke every single window on that car, including the mirrors, and I even put holes in the trunk with the claw part of the hammer. The whole time I was yelling his name at the top of my lungs, cursing, and telling him to stop playing with me! *The Jezebel Spirit had taken full and complete control!!!!*

I had never in my life been that angry. I could've been killed going to that woman's house. Oh, but my rant wasn't over, I called his wife and told her everything that had ever gone on or been said between us. Today, I regret my actions and behavior. My intentions were never to hurt her. My thought process was delusional and demonic. I was selfish, heartless, disrespectful, lacked self-control, and wanted to destroy him. If I could go back and undo the pain and embarrassment I caused that woman, I would.

When I left from destroying his car, he drove to my mother's house to let her know and see the damage I had done to his car. He was more worried about that car than me calling his wife. My mom told him he needed to leave me alone and to leave her property. There wasn't anything she could do. I was grown and had a mind of my own. I knew the potential consequences of my actions, but I did not care.

Today, I regret my actions and behavior. My intentions were never to hurt her.

You're probably thinking that was the end of our affair,

right? Wrong. About a month later, he called to tell me how much he missed me and asked if he could see me? I agreed and our affair continued, even after I'd told his wife about us and destroyed his car. I found out a few weeks later that I hadn't been the only other woman he was promising to be with. I found out about another girl who lived in a different county. I questioned him about her, and he adamantly denied her. He claimed it was nothing more than a conversation through Facebook messenger, said she wanted him, and even went as far as to give me the girl's address that she'd given to him.

I ended up speaking with her, and she told me how he had dogged me to her. He told her I was exaggerating the seriousness of our relationship. I was delusional, and I was obsessed with him. He told her it had just been sex between us, and I didn't mean anything to him. Listening to what she had to say, I disputed and rejected it, but deep down I knew the only thing good we had together was sex. Nothing more.... nothing less. I may have loved him, but he definitely didn't love me at all. He showed me that a few times. But to hear another woman tell me how he truly felt for me was harsh and damaging to my pride and my soul.

I was only a pawn in his game. He got what he could out of me sexually, financially, mentally, and emotionally. I meant nothing to him. I created this illusion in my head about a happily ever after with someone else's husband. I knew he was lying to me. I knew he couldn't be trusted. I knew he was a thief, and he had an addiction to sex. I knew it all, but I chose to stay in that mess!

I confronted him with everything she'd told me. Again, he denied it all and said she was just making things up to make it seem like it was something going on between them. I knew he was lying, but it made me feel better to hear him denying it all. A few short days later, the girl's ex-boyfriend messaged me on Facebook to tell me she and *that liar* went out of town together for the weekend. My heart dropped. He told me he was going out of town because his baby boy had a football game. I tried calling them both, only to get no answer from either of them, so I knew they were together.

The following Monday, I ended up texting that chic to vent my frustrations that not only did he lie about her, but she continued to entertain him, knowing he was fooling with me. Isn't that something? Again, my mindset was terrible. Three minutes later, she sent me picture texts of herself with the man I'd wasted 3 years having an affair with together. They were in a hotel room on the beach. In the pictures, he was smiling from ear to ear. It was as if he didn't have a care in the world, and there were two other women back in Knoxville who he was also misleading. Along with the picture texts, she captioned it *Eat your heart out.*

After 3 years of this sex driven affair, all of the drama, his broken promises, his lies, confusion, chaos, toxicity, him misleading me, and three long years of me waiting on this man to leave his wife to be with me, he was taking another female on trips and risking it all for her! That almost drove me over the edge. I already knew where the girl lived, and I called her child's father whom she'd betrayed also to be with *him.* I asked her child's father to confirm the address. I guess I was too calm or something, and he could feel the evil in my heart that I was trying to hide. He said, "No, Tameka! Don't do it. They're not worth it." He refused to confirm the address. I had made up in my mind and heart that I was going to drive to that county, knock on her door, shoot whoever opened it in the face, and make sure they were both dead before I left.

I was hurt, broken, angry, and felt I'd been used! He should've let me go all the times I tried to walk away. On top of all that, he was the reason my brother and I were no longer speaking. I was going to blow his head off for playing with my heart and all he'd put me through. Then, I planned to blow her head off for laughing at my pain. The scariest part is that neither one of them knew I was planning this. Even today, they have no clue how close they actually came to being on the front cover of the newspaper as victims of a double homicide. Before I ruined my life, I heard the Holy Spirit say, "How are you going to kill another woman's husband? What about the pain you inflicted upon her over Her own husband?" Then, I got a glimpse of myself sitting in prison serving a life sentence for double homicide away from my family. BUT GOD !!!!!!!!!!!!!!!!!!

After a few days had passed, I remember crying to my little brother Chris and expressing how much "He" had broken my heart. Suddenly, my brother said THE MOST PROFOUND AND IMPACTFUL THING THAT HE COULD'VE SAID TO ME, "No, Tameka! You broke your own heart, baby. You knew that man was married when you started messing with him. If he would betray his own wife, what made you think he'd treat you any differently?" Something inside of me clicked and reality sat in. I went on a fast, prayed, lay in the middle of my living room floor, and begged God to deliver me from that soul tie and to forgive me for everything I had done up until that point. I vowed to God that I would never again commit adultery. I would never look at another woman's husband in that way, and I meant it. I watched Bishop Noel Jones every day, all day, read the Bible, and released my pain to God.

God in His faithfulness, goodness, mercy, and forgiveness delivered me, and I never dealt with that man again. A couple of months went by after all of that, and he reached out to me, wanting to come see me. He said, "I miss you and I replied, "The devil is a lie. Hell no!" Then, I hung up in his face." I haven't spoken to nor seen him since and that was almost five years ago. He eventually left his wife. They got divorced, and he ended up with that other chic he had denied to me, but it turns out he didn't treat her any differently from his first wife or me for that matter. She's just taking the place of the women he nearly destroyed. Along with that replacement came a lot of lies, cheating, and heartache.

He's still the lying, cheating, womanizing human being

that he's always been. I heard he ended up fathering another child with someone else since he's been with her. Although she took pleasure in my pain, I do not take any in hers. I actually feel sorry for her and pray she finds the strength to get out one day too. As I see it now, she did me favor, and I sincerely thank her for it, from the bottom of my heart!

See the spirit of Jezebel is persistent. It's a destroyer, a murderous, lying, perverse, thieving demonic force from the pits of hell, and you're no match for it in the flesh. **You've got to literally fight it in the spirit!!!!** You first have to recognize it, call it out, denounce it, pray against it, and fast!

I went on a fast. I lay in my living room floor and begged God to deliver and forgive me for having an affair with a married man. Bishop Noel Jones and Bishop T.D Jakes stayed on my T.V. screen every day for a while. I was determined to be delivered from that thang. Hallelujah, I was!! I'm here to witness to any young lady out there who is either in an extramarital affair or if you're ever faced with one. If you're already in it, *please get out of it!* If you're thinking about having one or a married man approaches you, *please don't do it!*

It's wrong in The sight of God, and it can have deadly consequences. You will also reap what you sow!! If he'll cheat on his wife to be with you, he'll cheat on you to be with the next woman. *No good thing will come of it. It's already cursed!* You must understand and always remember **God honors marriage, and he's never going to send you another woman's husband!!!!**

I wasn't in the will of God, and I definitely wasn't walking in God's purpose for my life during that time. I didn't have a relationship with God. I knew Him, but I had gotten distracted and wandered so far away from Him. The woman I am today would never engage in causing another woman harm or damage to a sacred union. I'm not perfect, but I thrive daily to live for God now. May this chapter and my experience help someone and spare you a lot of disappointment, heartache, and pain. TO GOD BE THE GLORY FOR DELIVERANCE!!!!

The Season of Separation and Self-Accountability

CHAPTER 13

It was 4:01 A.M. on 3/16/2022. I couldn't sleep. That was the night I attempted to type this final chapter. I typed and erased for 3 hours.

When I first started writing this book, I already had it in my mind what this chapter was going to be about. I was going to talk about my marriage and what lead to our separation. I was going to write about everything I had to endure, how I was hurt, betrayed, and more. When I began writing, I clearly heard God say, "this chapter is not about your husband's shortcomings, faults, or flaws during your marriage. It's about yours! My purpose for you writing this chapter of the book is for you to help lead, guide, and teach others what you've learned about what it is to be a wife, not just any wife, a kingdom wife! I'll deal with him in my way, for my way is better than yours!"

My biggest intentions for writing this entire book was to glorify God, to show His goodness, grace, and mercy for me throughout my life. So, here I am totally submissive, transparent, and walking in obedience to what the Father has instructed me to do. I had never been a wife. Not only had I never been a wife, I didn't know what it was to be a Kingdom wife. I came into our marriage with a lot of baggage, unhealed past trauma, a lot of deeply rooted hurt, hidden unforgiveness, soul draining anger, and toxicity. I entered it with 42 years worth of unhealthy mental emotional weight I never sought counseling for. I had suppressed and carried those things around inside of me for far too long. Therefore, I have to take accountability for the breakdown of my marriage.

I married my husband while he was still in federal prison. He was serving a 10-year prison sentence when we got together. We were together his last three years of that sentence. I didn't realize the patience it required to be married to someone who was accustomed to certain ways of doing things, thinking, and acting. Bless his heart, he was institutionalized, and I would, at times, throw that in his face. Looking back, he had to be scared out of his mind to come home to a city and a society where things had changed dramatically during his 10-year incarceration. If he made the slightest mistake, he could have been sent back, never to see the light of day again due to the three strike law.

All he had that was familiar and safe to him was me and his family. They had even changed tremendously as far as age and health. I wasn't patient enough with him, and I was controlling. At times, I'm sure he probably felt he was still being guarded. I would get so angry with my husband that I was verbally and sometimes physically abusive towards him. Instead of building him up, I would tear him down whenever I felt hurt or neglected. Instead of me praying for him, over him, and about whatever was concerning me, I tried to control the outcome of the situations on my own.

> I battled depression like never before,

I was also afraid of being hurt, betrayed, and let down. My fear was so great that I allowed it to control my thinking, which my thinking then caused me to speak certain things out of my mouth and into existence. Our separation taught me something. Although I'd physically overcome every past trauma, I had not overcome them all emotionally, mentally, or spiritually. It took God allowing my marriage to completely break down and Him putting me in total isolation with Him for me to clearly see *me*. This is not about me taking ALL OF THE BLAME. It's about me taking full accountability for my part. The other accountability is between God and my husband.

When we first separated nine months ago, I was extremely resentful, bitter, and hurt. I felt abandoned, betrayed, played, and used! I cried myself to sleep so many nights, wondering why God allowed it to happen. I battled depression like never before, only getting out of bed most days because of my oldest granddaughter who lives with me. I didn't understand anything. I just wanted to shut down because I was angry with God. I didn't want talk to Him. I didn't want to praise, read His word, or anything else.

I thank God for the spiritual leaders He placed in my life

during this season and the amazing women's weekly check-in group. These ladies were from my church and other cities and states. Iron sharpens iron, and I gained a lot of strength from them. I had also gotten into counseling and started dealing with things through professional therapy. I learned I was still holding on to parts of a past relationship and expecting certain things from my husband that I received in that past relationship. That was not fair to him at all. It was wrong, unfair, and basically setting him up for failure because every person is different, and they love in their own way. I should've released old experiences and embraced the new, especially with my husband.

Another mistake I made was being too controlling. If you don't have trust, you don't have anything. Although you're married, you still have individuality, and you've got to trust your husband enough to be his own individual self, separate from you. I was so caught up in what my husband was or wasn't doing right that I couldn't see myself, and I was too full of strife that I couldn't hear from God. Sometimes God will separate you from people and put you in a place of isolation so you can't do anything but call on Him. I was too wrapped up in my husband and was not making time for God.

We have to remember that God's name is jealous. He's a jealous God and will not come second to anyone or anything. You must keep him first and before all things !!!!! You see, the separation was necessary for my spiritual growth! God had to deal with me alone. He needed me to let go of some things that were hindering my walk with him, so I had to go through a painful crushing and an excruciating pruning. God had to cut some things away from me so that I may be fruitful!!!

My branches weren't bearing the right fruits. I had a cursing tongue, an angry spirit, and an unforgiving heart. I was controlling, jealous, and insecure. I was loud, disrespectful, defiant, unyielding, bitter, and spiteful in nature! I had to learn how to first be submissive to God before I could ever be submissive to my husband.

At the beginning of my separation, I was still refusing to fully submit to God. I was fighting my emotions. I wouldn't allow myself to cry or feel the affliction that was upon me. I tried to avoid processing and seeing my faults and imperfections. Oh, but God has a way of breaking you all the way down to the point where you have no choice but to submit unto Him. It was during that time that I felt I had been stripped naked, weak, helpless, powerless, and I had no choice but to lay my heart down at the Throne of God and surrender myself to HIM.

I had no peace. My thoughts were constantly racing. My imagination was all over the place, and I was becoming more bitter, impatient, and discouraged. I was in a dark place, and depression had a grip on me. At one point, I even felt, *Why should I keep glorifying a God who would allow His child to hurt like this?* I wanted to give up and say forget it. Some days I didn't care if I lived or died. I was tired of going through adversity after adversity, test after test, disappointment after disappointment, and now I've been dealt this hand after all the good I had done.

I was on my soap box and throwing a tantrum because GOD wasn't moving as fast as I wanted. I felt I was being punished while my husband was out here living his best life, and I was angry as hell with God for allowing it. During this time, I was off work on medical leave from having a hip replacement. I felt abandoned and hurt that my husband wasn't there to care for me, so that mental pain on top of my physical pain only intensified everything.

Because of the opiate crisis, the surgeon prescribed me Percocet (5 milligrams) for pain. Due to my body weight alone, those were definitely not strong enough for my physical pain nor were they strong enough to make me feel better mentally about life in general, but he refused to write me anything stronger. I was in terrible physical pain, and I took it upon myself to buy some off the streets. After the pain had subsided, I found myself still buying and taking them. It was not to help with the physical pain but to help me feel better mentally and emotionally.

The pills gave me a false sense of peace and motivation that I was going to be okay. Literally, my third time buying some, the Holy Spirit came to me and said, "Do you not see what is happening? You are out of the will of God and back on the road to destruction, if you do not stop now!!!" The pills I had just taken did not have any effect on me whatsoever, and I literally became sick to my stomach!!

That day, I cut it off instantly. I did not buy another pill. I repented, and thanked him for blocking that attempted assassination on my life! I call it an attempted assassination because fentanyl is literally killing folks every day on the streets. People are dropping like flies from getting a hold of pain medication laced with it! You're literally playing russian roulette when you buy drugs off the streets!

I am responsible for the influence I have and the example I set for those who have been following my journey over the years, those who have witnessed GOD'S POWER in my life and who find strength, encouragement, and hope for their struggles by watching my walk with God. They have followed and watched me while God delivered me from drugs, prostitution, and other things. It is imperative that I represent my Father to the best of my ability so that they may be led to Christ for deliverance! To God be the glory for blocking the trick of the enemy and for allowing me to hearken to the voice of the holy spirit!

Just that fast, the enemy found an opening and was luring me back down that dark path. How was I writing a book about how God delivered me from drugs, testifying, and witnessing, and behind closed doors I was taking medicine not prescribed to me? One thing about God, He will not let anyone make a mockery of Him!!! I have an assignment, a purpose, a calling, an oil, a mantle over my life, and I can't afford to let anything distract me or get me off course! In this separation, I've not only learned a lot, but I've grown tremendously, I'm better because of it, and I'm now more fruitful than ever before.

I loved the ground my husband walked on, and I still love

him very much. I'm no longer angry nor resentful of him for his transgressions against me. Whether we reconcile or finally end up getting divorced, I wish him the absolute best, all the happiness, and love in the world. He's a good person. He has his ways, and prayerfully he'll recognize and work on them to become an even better person, a mighty man of God. I pray he'll become that marriage counselor he wants to be.

The few people who know and love me on a personal level will read this and say, "No, it wasn't all your fault," or they may feel I let him off too easily, but that's just it. It's not about me letting him off too easily. This is about me releasing, healing, owning, growing, and walking in obedience to God. I should've never started talking about my husband's shortcomings to anyone but God because when and if the time ever comes that God allows us to reconcile, we will move on while others will never forget what he did or what he said.

I'd like to pass along some advice to newly married wives.

1) Pray over, for, and with your husband!!!

Keep him covered at all times. Temptation is real. The schemes of the enemy are real, but your prayers will keep him covered!!

2) Ladies don't talk outside of your household about what's going between you and your husband. Keep family and close friends out of your marriage.

3) Ladies respect your husband, even if and when you do not agree, respect him.

Never tear him down or emasculate him, especially in front of someone!

4) If you have thoughts or ideas about how a man is supposed to be or how to love you based off of past relationships, get rid of them!

They are not the same person, and it isn't fair. If he doesn't meet those expectations, it'll leave

> Never tear him down or emasculate him, especially in front of someone!

you feeling disappointed, which will in turn cause you to hold it against your husband. I'm not saying don't set standards for yourself because every woman knows how she deserves to be treated. I'm simply saying, "Let your husband be himself!"

5) Be quick to forgive. Let go of your pride and forgive. If you're wrong, ask for forgiveness. Nothing destroys love quicker than pride.

6) Times will get hard. You won't always like your spouse. At times you may feel like giving up and walking out on your marriage but stand! Pray and stand!!!!

7) never lose yourself. Keep yourself up!!! The same way we want the man to keep chasing us long after he gets us, keep giving him something to chase long after he gets you!

I started my weight loss journey. So far, I've lost 41lbs and counting. I don't just want to look better. I want to feel better physically, emotionally, mentally, and spiritually. Confidence is sexy. Confidence is beautiful. Confidence comes from knowing who you are in Christ Jesus!!! I am working towards being the absolute best version of me that I can be!!!!!

Unfortunately, my marriage ended in a divorce. Out of this fire, I have been built into a kingdom wife. This is the power that will help me to move forward. This is not the end of my story it is only the end of this chapter of my life.

To be continued....

God and Tameka Smith!

About the Author
Tameka Smith

Tameka Smith is a native of Knoxville, Tennessee. She is a speaker, author, mentor, and motivator who is passionate about helping others transform and triumph over their trauma. Tameka is the proud mother of three amazing children and five dynamic grandchildren.

She is a nontraditional minister of the gospel who has taken the pulpit wherever God graced her feet. Over the past eight years, as a public transit operator in Knoxville, God has allowed her to daily minister to and mentor homeless people, those who suffer with mental illness, and those who struggle with substance abuse. When she is not preaching in her nontraditional pulpit, by invitation, she occasionally shares her testimony in local churches. Tameka's deepest desire is to fulfill the great commission by going into all nations preaching the gospel of Jesus Christ, as God uses the power of her testimony to draw men unto Him.

Tameka is on the path of pursuing her dream of starting a spiritual outreach program, to mentor and help troubled teen girls and women who are broken, battered, and substance abusers. Tameka desires to see them thrive beyond their trauma and live the life of their dreams through pursuing their purpose in God. In the future, she is looking forward to releasing another book and producing a movie based on her life's story so that God can continue to be gloried.

Finally, Ms. Smith has decided to make herself available to motivate others as a spiritual motivational speaker. Feel free to contact her for your next event so that your attendees can have a transformational encounter.

Contact Information

Email Address: tamekachareesesmith@gmail.com

Social Media: Tameka Smith